The End Is Near...Or Maybe Not!

The End Is Near...Or Maybe Not!

by

Kenneth N. Myers

Mayeux Press

SHERMAN, TEXAS

The End Is Near...Or Maybe Not!

Myers, Kenneth Neal, 1959-
The End Is Near...Or Maybe Not! Kenneth N. Myers

1. Christian Eschatology 2. Theology

Dewey Decimal Classification: 236

Cover design: Neal Mayeux
Cover painting: *The Destruction of Jerusalem*, Nicolas Poussin,
c. 1640.

Published by Mayeux Press
561 Bailey Drive, Denison, TX 75021

"Eschatology is important...but it's not the end of the world."
-Canon Mark Pearson

Acknowledgements

This book is dedicated to Allen and Karen Wienke, who encouraged a young pastor to study out what he believed about eschatology, and to teach them as he learned, and to the Reverend Donald W. Ross, who harassed that same young pastor with the truth.

Thank you to the congregation of Christ Church Cathedral, who have afforded me the opportunity to write, and have supported me in teaching this material before it was ever set down on the page.

As always, thank you to my wife Shirley who is always supportive, and graciously endures my writing trips, patiently waiting for my occasional breaks.

Thank you to Tom at *Hotel Luz en Yucatan* in Merida, Mexico, who provided a peaceful haven for writing.

Table of Contents

Preface
2012 And All That

Ask yourself a question. How many times have you heard people speak with heartfelt conviction that the end was imminent? As the year 2000 approached? In the last few years? Now ask yourself another question. Were *any* of them right? Even close?

I'm sitting here in Merida, Yucatan, Mexico, working on this book. It is January, 2012. Yes — THE 2012 — the year the Mayan Calendar ends. And I am in the heart of Mayan country. Chichen Itza is just down the highway from me. *Chicken Pibil* is just down the street (but, I digress). Mexico is having troubles right now, and thousands of people are murdered every year in the ongoing drug wars, but Merida is safe. It has been recognized as the third safest city in the world, with only one murder recorded for the whole year of 2011. Still, tourism in Merida and all of Mexico has been down in recent years. In 2011 there were 22 million tourists in Mexico. But, in 2012, they are expecting 52 million tourists! More than double the normal amount of gringos are going to be heading to Mexico this year, and the largest part of them to the Yucatan Peninsula, because...get this...it is 2012! The Mayan Calendar ends on December 21, 2012 and people want to celebrate the year before the end of the world arrives. Of course, these partiers and revelers aren't really expecting the end of all things; they're more expecting a good time, a pretty beach, warm weather and a chance to check out the Mayan ruins. But seriously, more than double the tourist crowd because of the Mayan Calendar? Here's the point: people, run-of-the-mill heathens, but especially Christians, are *fascinated* with the approaching end of the world.

I'm betting the world won't end in 2012. I also bet that it wouldn't end in 2011 when Harold Camping was making his predictions of the Rapture occurring in May. Instead of selling everything we had, our church folk had an "End of the World Party"—we cooked out burgers, had some good fellowship, and listened to some appropriate music (*Don't They Know It's The End of the World?* by the Carpenters, *It's The End of the World As We Know It* by R.E.M., and *Apocalypso* by Jimmy Buffett).

In fact, I'm betting the end won't come in my lifetime or yours. We have work to do first. On the following pages I will unfold a biblical, historic, sane, sensible, and hopeful view of the future.

Introduction

What You Should Know
Before We Dig In

Where I Come From

In 1981, I was convinced the Rapture would arrive before the end of the year. I was 22 years old, the son of an Assemblies of God minister, and had been mesmerized by "the end times" since I was 12. I had gone to conferences with my father, and while he buddied around with his pastor friends, I had sat through lectures by the movers and shakers of my theological word, explaining how Israel's restoration as a nation in 1948 was the lighting of the fuse for "the terminal generation," and how we had less than 40 years before the Second Coming, and seven years less than that before the secret Rapture which would rescue the remnant of true Christians from the impending chaos of the Great Tribulation and all that nasty stuff like the mark of the beast and the fiery hailstones and the giant stinging scorpions—we mustn't forget the giant stinging scorpions. The Second Coming: no later than 1988; the Rapture: no later than 1981. I heard one preacher say, "If it doesn't happen, I'll eat my Bible."

I believed this teaching with all my heart. At the age of 12 I was helping my father study for his sermons on Revelation (or, as I said back then, "Revelations"), scouring through an old and worn out copy of the big brown square book, *Dispensational Truth* by Clarence Larkin. I memorized the maps and charts and spent hours piecing together the complicated puzzle of strange beasts and dragons and harlots and bowls of wrath. As a young adolescent, I fully believed that I would never have the chance to get married, I would never experience sex, I would never have children, I would never finish college, I would never have a career. Jesus was coming, at the latest, four years after I graduated from high school.

By the time I began ministry as an assistant pastor in South Texas, I knew eschatology (that's the 29 cent word for "the study of last things") like the back of my hand. I had read every book on the subject that I could get my hands on—all of Hal Lindsay's books, John Walvoord, C.I. Scofield's Study Bible, John Hall's massive charts, Charles Ryrie, Lewis Sperry Chaffer—you name it, I had read it.

Naturally, as a young assistant pastor (I began at the age of 19—*shudder!*) half of my teaching leaned in the direction of my favorite study. The end times was a big topic on the campus of my Bible School—one fellow quit after the first year because Jesus was coming back, and he didn't need to be wasting his time in preparation—*there was no time to prepare*—he had to get out there and beat the spiritual pavement and save souls while it was still day, because the night was just around the corner, when no one could work.

In the first six years of ministry, I taught through the book of Revelation twice in the same church in an adult Sunday School class. I preached on the impending catastrophes. I talked about the signs of the times over coffee with parishioners. Then everything I believed in started to fall apart.

The Unraveling

My first clue that I was in trouble came from an old Church of Christ minister serving in the same town I was in — Zapata, Texas. We had monthly pastoral meetings, and old Johnny Johnson was always there. For years he had been writing a weekly column for the local paper, and he wrote a rather detailed series on the book of Revelation and Matthew 24 (the "Little Apocalypse," as some call it). And what he said was completely off the charts. It made no sense. I felt sorry for this old guy who had pastored so many years but was so ignorant of "present day truths!" I've always wished I could see Johnny face to face now and apologize for thinking he was crazy.

The second thread began unraveling as a result of reading C.S. Lewis. I had started reading him while I was in high school, but didn't get to the third book of his *Space Trilogy* until I was preparing for ministry. The most profound of the three books, the last one, *That Hideous Strength*, dealt with the end of the world. My goodness, I had admired Lewis all through the Narnia books, I had learned so much from *Mere Christianity*. How could this intellectual Christian hero of mine be so, well, *ignorant*—when it came to eschatology? I finished the book and thought to myself, this brilliant man completely misses everything about the end! Where's the seven year tribulation? Where's the millennium? Where's the mark of the beast? And, dang it, where are the stinging scorpions?

The Final Straw

The straw that broke the camel's back was when one of my old college professors (and a dear friend of mine), Donald Ross, informed me that he no longer believed like we always had. I thought Don had joined the ranks of Johnny Johnson and C.S. Lewis and had signed up for membership in the *We Don't Have A Clue About Eschatology Club*. But Don started sending me books, and letters, and we had long phone conversations, and little by little he chiseled away at my firm and pat dispensational way of thinking.

At the age of 25, while pastoring a small congregation in rural Northwestern Wisconsin, I walked into the church for our Wednesday evening Bible study (yes—my third pass-through of Revelation—I was about six weeks into the study) and told that poor, shell-shocked flock, "You know everything

I've been teaching for the last six weeks? Well, I don't believe *any* of it!"

"What *do* you believe?" they asked.

"I don't know," I responded, "I simply know what I do *not* believe. Give me a year to dig in and study, and I'll get back to you on the matter."

"Well, why don't we take a year and all dig in together?" was their response. So we did. That was 1984, and I haven't looked back since.

Where I'm Going

This book does not pretend to answer every question anyone could possibly have about eschatology. Neither does it attempt to be a deep scholarly account which theologians will peruse for years to come. Scholarly accounts already exist, and some of them are exceedingly valuable, but these don't get read by the average person. It seems to me there are three possible categories for a book on eschatology to fall into. At the top of the list is the scholarly, heavy, and unread-by-the-people books. At the bottom of the list are the popular novels and studies which people seem to gobble up but which are completely wrong. What I am attempting to write is a readable, solid, biblical and understandable study of an eschatology of hope and victory which will be both enjoyable and mind-changing. When you have finished this book, if it has whetted your appetite and you want to do more reading, I will suggest some of those good scholarly books for your ongoing study.

Chapter One
The Battle of the Views

Did you read the preface and introduction? They are both short and important. I'm not going to write any more until you go back and read them. They will only take a few minutes. The rest of us will wait here for you.

OK. Thank you for humoring me. See, I told you they would be short and important. Now, on with the book.

Three Main Views

When it comes to talking about biblical eschatology, there are three main views, all of which take their lead from a little phrase in Revelation 20: "1000 years." The Latin word for 1000 years is *millennium*, and the three views each have a different understanding regarding this 1000 year period of time which St. John refers to. All three views fall within orthodox Christian belief. The Apostles' Creed says, "He shall come again to judge the living and the dead." The Nicene Creed says, "He shall come again, with glory, to judge both the living and the dead, and his kingdom shall have no end." Both creeds affirm the resurrection of the body. These things must be believed to be within the fold of sound Christian faith. Beyond this, whichever of these three millennium views you hold, you will find yourself in good and godly company.

Postmillennialism: Folk who hold to this view believe that Jesus comes again *after* (hence, "post") the millennium. They believe that the Gospel will go forward, reach a point of virtual success, and then there will be a 1000 year period of everything being wonderful, which will culminate with the Second Coming of Christ, Judgment Day and the New Creation. This view has waxed and waned through the years, and finds its largest base among conservative Presbyterian and Reformed believers.

Premillennialism: Yep, you guessed it: people who hold this view believe that Jesus will return *before* the millennium. He will come back, set up his kingdom on earth, and rule from Jerusalem for 1000 years. After the 1000 years are over, there will be a final rebellion, God and the saints will whip up on the bad guys, Judgment Day will ensue, and the New Creation will come to pass.

Now, to complicate things just a little: there are two camps in the Premillennialist nation. The first camp is called **historic premillennialism** and it believes basically what I just described above. You will find these folk scattered throughout the church world, from Baptist and Methodist to Presbyterian and Anglican and all points between. The second camp is called **dispensational premillennialism**, and it has much more complicated charts and graphs.

Here, in a simplified run-down, is what these Christians believe:

1. A secret Rapture occurs, when Christians meet Jesus in the air, are lifted off the earth, and go away to heaven, physically, for seven years.
2. After the Rapture, a seven year period known as "The Great Tribulation" occurs on the Christianless earth, during which the Antichrist deceives the whole world into following him, kills anyone who converts to Christ during this time, sets himself up as a deity to be worshiped, becomes the world dictator, and generally makes life miserable for the Jews.
3. During this Great Tribulation all hell breaks loose. There are massive wars, terrible famines, catastrophic natural disasters, plagues of all kinds, and really big stinging scorpions—I just don't like those stinging scorpions.
4. At the end of this seven year Tribulation, Jesus comes again—the first time he didn't actually come back to earth, he just came to the air and caught up the believers—kind of a drive-by Rapture. But at the end of the Tribulation he comes back all the way to the *terra firma*—this is the *real* Second Coming —defeats the Antichrist and his minions, binds Satan in chains of darkness, raises

from the dead those who had converted to Christ during the Tribulation (a massive revival happens among the Jews after the Christians are already gone), and sets up his Kingdom with the capitol being Jerusalem. Oh—and he brings back all the saints who had gone away with him in the Rapture.

5. After the Second Coming, Jesus rules and reigns, along with his resurrected saints, for 1000 years. Things are really good during this time. The saints, obviously, are already immortal—a kind of undying ruling class, but there are mortals left who survived the Tribulation, the Battle of Armageddon, and the Second Coming. These folk continue living normal lives, having children, going to jobs, building houses, and eventually dying. But they live to be really old—maybe even a thousand years old.

6. At the end of this 1000 year reign of Christ, Satan is loosed, and convinces most of the mortal people—who have enjoyed unheard of longevity and peace under the benevolent rule of Christ and his saints—to rebel against God, and there is one last massive battle where they are all destroyed.

7. Finally, Judgment day comes, when everyone—believers who died during the millennium and non-believers who died any time in the history of the world from Adam to the end—rise from the dead and stand

before God for a final judgment. The wicked are thrown into the Lake of Fire forever and the righteous enjoy the New Creation forever.

This latter view was the view I was raised with and believed my first 24 years of life. I am thoroughly convinced it is a novel view (it didn't exist until the 1830s) and doesn't square up with the Bible. But, man! It makes for exciting fiction, popular bestsellers, cool charts, and third rate movies. This is the view of Hal Lindsay's *The Late Great Planet Earth* and Tim LaHaye's & Jerry Jenkins' *Left Behind* series. This view is usually found among Southern Baptists, Non-denominational Charismatic congregations, Bible Churches, and the Assemblies of God.

Amillennialism: Finally, there are people who believe the 1000 years referred to in the Revelation are simply symbolic. They aren't to be taken literally, and this time period refers to the whole time between the First Coming of Christ as a baby in Bethlehem and the Second Coming of Christ as King of Kings and Lord of Lords on the Last Day. This view has a simple timeline with Jesus going up at the Ascension and coming down on the Last Day, which is also Judgment Day and the final establishing of the New Creation. Even if this view might turn out to be wrong, its chart is a lot easier to draw.

Two Attitudes

Now that we have briefly explored the three millennial views, I need to add another aspect of how we look at future things. We see the future either from a basically pessimistic view or a basically optimistic view. Postmillennialism is obviously optimistic. Dispensational Premillennialism is obviously pessimistic. Historic Premillennialists and Amillennialists can fall into either group. Some Amillennialists are almost as pessimistic as the Dispensationalists. Some are as hopeful as the Postmillennialists.

One way of looking at this whole matter is to ask a question: "Is the Great Commission *do-able*?" In the last three verses of the Gospel of Matthew, the Risen Christ gives orders to his followers: "All authority in heaven and on earth has been given to me. Go therefore and make disciples of all nations, baptizing them in the name of the Father and of the Son and of the Holy Spirit, teaching them to observe all that I have commanded you. And behold, I am with you always, to the end of the age." (Matthew 28.18-20).

Can this actually happen? Can the Spirit-empowered Church actually succeed in this job-description and mission given to her by her Lord? Can she really make disciples of the nations? Can she really instruct the nations to obey Christ? Eschatological pessimists say, "No." When it is all said and done, only a remnant of people will actually believe; a minority. Eschatological optimists say, "Yes!" Sure, there is a ton of work to be done, and we have a long way to go, and it won't all be smooth sailing, but God's biddings are his enablings. When it is all said and done, the nations will walk in the splendor of His glory, and in *every place*, from the rising of the sun to the going down of the same, His name shall be great *among the nations*, and incense and a pure offering will be offered to his Name. Thus was the hope of the Prophets (Revelation 21.24, Malachi 1.11) and thus is the hope of the Church.

And Now I Show My Cards

If you haven't guessed by now, the ideas presented in this book will be from an Amillennialist view—that there is no literal 1000 years at the end of history, but that the Church Age *is* that 1000 years (there will be an entire chapter on this later), and from an optimistic view—that the Church will actually accomplish what Jesus commissioned her to do. The end doesn't come with a bang. It doesn't come with a whimper, either. It comes with victory.

"But, if this is true," you might be saying (and you might already be hoping it *is* true), "Then what about all the nasty stuff? What about 'The Great Tribulation' and the Antichrist and all that goes with it? Did you do something tricky and just conveniently ignore it and make that disappear?" Nope, no tricks here. I've just shown you all my cards. In the coming pages I'm going to (hopefully) offer a convincing argument that all the nasty things in Matthew 24, the book of the Revelation, and other passages, are *first century occurrences*. Contrary to Johnny Cash's song, Matthew 24 is *not* knocking at your door. It knocked at the door of Jerusalem in A.D. 70.

Why Should I Care About The Future?

I have a lot of pastor friends who don't know what they believe about the future. They honestly don't even want to explore it, because everything they have studied so far seems to them foggy and confusing. The deeper they get the foggier it gets. Many of them have already abandoned a strict Dispensationalist view, but are comfortably uncomfortable with saying, "I don't know how it will all turn out, so I'll just serve Jesus and wait and see."

This is a relatively safe approach, and certainly easier than having to wrestle for themselves with heavy eschatological issues. But there are two problems with this attitude.

First, it isn't biblical. My goodness! Jesus and Paul and John and Peter and Matthew and Mark and Luke and Jude and James and whoever wrote Hebrews all talked about it. So did Moses and David and Jeremiah and Ezekiel and Isaiah and Daniel and Malachi (I have to stop here...too much typing!). How can we, as people faithful to the Word of God, simply ignore or put on a shelf something that is so significantly present in the whole of Scripture? If we are going to be faithful servants, ably handling the Word of God, we have to come to grips with these issues.

Second, *the future determines the past*. Yes, I'll say it again, the future determines the past. What I mean is this. If you and I make plans to go on a picnic next Thursday, that future event determines what we do before it arrives.

We have to decide where to go. Someone has to bring the sandwiches. Someone needs to get the wine. Will there be a blanket to sit on? How will we deal with the ants? Plans must be made, or else the picnic might not happen at all!

Similarly, what we expect about the "big" future determines what we do before it arrives. Is Jesus coming back to rescue a few who are holding the fort awaiting his arrival? Then our best option is to dig in, save as many souls as we can, expect things to get worse, forget about transforming society, and hold on for dear life. But if Jesus is coming back to the welcome of a victorious church, then we have work to do; things like making disciples of the nations (not just a few *in* the nations), teaching the world to obey everything Jesus has commanded us, saving souls—yes—but also transforming cultures, influencing economics, recovering the arts, channeling technology toward godly goals, and a whole host of other things. If Jesus is coming back really soon, we don't need to send people to seminary—there isn't time for that. If he's coming back after we have accomplished our purposes, then we have time on our side—send a kid to seminary and prepare him for a life of ministry, train up children to be good parents and grandparents, elect godly leaders, write books, and plant trees, for God's sake (literally).

When the ancient cathedrals were being built in Europe, the Christians understood that it might take a hundred or more years to complete them. When the foundations were laid, forests of trees were planted to serve as scaffolding a generation later. Stonemasons trained their sons to follow them in the trade and multiple generations of families made their living working on the church. One cathedral in England took a thousand years to finish! But it's been finished for five hundred years and is still used for the worship of God. This is a far cry from throwing up a tin building in the hopes that it will last 20 years until Jesus comes.

The future determines the past. What do *you* believe about the future?

Chapter Two
The Last Days

Thlipsis! *Te thlipsis*, even! This is the Greek word that gets translated *trouble, suffering, oppression, affliction, persecution,* and — are you ready, *tribulation*! And, oh my goodness, the *thlipsis* that the word *thlipsis* has caused for Bible students over the years.

The word is found in several places in the Bible, but the most significant is in Jesus' teachings in Matthew 24. What I intend to show is that what Matthew 24 is not about an end-times global "Great Tribulation" which is preceded by the Rapture of the Saints and whose prime figure is the Antichrist (by the way, take a wild guess at how many times the word Antichrist is used in Matthew 24 and the whole book of Revelation combined. None. Nada. Zip. It is used *only* in the epistles of

John—but more about that later). People who approach this "little apocalypse" (as Matthew 24 is sometimes called) with a predisposed understanding that it is talking about end-of-the-world events will quite honestly anticipate a future of horror rather than hope. I intend, in the next several chapters, to relocate "the Great Tribulation" to the first century after Christ, and to show that it is primarily a localized event, centering on Israel, and specifically on the city of Jerusalem.

What God Warned Israel About

To grasp the meaning of Matthew 24, it would do us well to go back to Deuteronomy 28, when God affirms his covenant with Israel, and notice the *negative sanctions*—the *curses*—which God says will befall Israel if she is not faithful to do all that he has commanded her. Mind you, God is speaking to his own chosen people here: people he has delivered from the bondage of Egypt and made his own and planted in a new, promised, land.

I know, when reading a book like this, that some people tend to skip over the long biblical passages referenced, but this one is important, so I'm putting it here in full. Take time to read it. It is the foundation of much of which is to follow.

15 "But if you will not obey the voice of the LORD your God or be careful to do all his commandments and his statutes that I command you today, then all these curses shall come upon you and overtake you. 16 Cursed shall you be in the city, and cursed shall you be in the field. 17 Cursed shall be your basket and your kneading bowl. 18 Cursed shall be the fruit of your womb and the fruit of your ground, the increase of your herds and the young of your flock. 19 Cursed shall you be when you come in, and cursed shall you be when you go out.
20 "The LORD will send on you curses, confusion, and frustration in all that you undertake to do, until you are destroyed and perish quickly on account of the evil of your deeds, because you have forsaken me. 21 The LORD will make the pestilence stick to you until he has consumed you off the land that you are entering to take possession of it. 22 The LORD will strike you with wasting disease and with fever, inflammation and fiery heat, and with drought and with blight and with mildew. They shall pursue you until you perish. 23 And the heavens over your head shall be bronze, and the earth under you shall be

iron. 24 The LORD will make the rain of your land powder. From heaven dust shall come down on you until you are destroyed.

25 "The LORD will cause you to be defeated before your enemies. You shall go out one way against them and flee seven ways before them. And you shall be a horror to all the kingdoms of the earth. 26 And your dead body shall be food for all birds of the air and for the beasts of the earth, and there shall be no one to frighten them away. 27 The LORD will strike you with the boils of Egypt, and with tumors and scabs and itch, of which you cannot be healed. 28 The LORD will strike you with madness and blindness and confusion of mind,29 and you shall grope at noonday, as the blind grope in darkness, and you shall not prosper in your ways. And you shall be only oppressed and robbed continually, and there shall be no one to help you. 30 You shall betroth a wife, but another man shall ravish her. You shall build a house, but you shall not dwell in it. You shall plant a vineyard, but you shall not enjoy its fruit. 31 Your ox shall be slaughtered before your eyes, but you shall not eat any of it. Your donkey shall be seized before your face, but shall not be restored to you. Your sheep shall be given to your enemies, but

there shall be no one to help you. 32 Your sons and your daughters shall be given to another people, while your eyes look on and fail with longing for them all day long, but you shall be helpless. 33 A nation that you have not known shall eat up the fruit of your ground and of all your labors, and you shall be only oppressed and crushed continually, 34 so that you are driven mad by the sights that your eyes see. 35 The LORD will strike you on the knees and on the legs with grievous boils of which you cannot be healed, from the sole of your foot to the crown of your head.

36 "The LORD will bring you and your king whom you set over you to a nation that neither you nor your fathers have known. And there you shall serve other gods of wood and stone. 37 And you shall become a horror, a proverb, and a byword among all the peoples where the LORD will lead you away. 38 You shall carry much seed into the field and shall gather in little, for the locust shall consume it. 39 You shall plant vineyards and dress them, but you shall neither drink of the wine nor gather the grapes, for the worm shall eat them. 40 You shall have olive trees throughout all your territory, but you shall not anoint yourself with the oil, for your

olives shall drop off. 41 You shall father sons and daughters, but they shall not be yours, for they shall go into captivity. 42 The cricket shall possess all your trees and the fruit of your ground. 43 The sojourner who is among you shall rise higher and higher above you, and you shall come down lower and lower. 44 He shall lend to you, and you shall not lend to him. He shall be the head, and you shall be the tail.

45 "All these curses shall come upon you and pursue you and overtake you till you are destroyed, because you did not obey the voice of the LORD your God, to keep his commandments and his statutes that he commanded you. 46 They shall be a sign and a wonder against you and your offspring forever. 47 Because you did not serve the LORD your God with joyfulness and gladness of heart, because of the abundance of all things, 48therefore you shall serve your enemies whom the LORD will send against you, in hunger and thirst, in nakedness, and lacking everything. And he will put a yoke of iron on your neck until he has destroyed you. 49 The LORD will bring a nation against you from far away, from the end of the earth, swooping down like the eagle, a nation whose language you do not understand, 50 a

hard-faced nation who shall not respect the old or show mercy to the young. 51 It shall eat the offspring of your cattle and the fruit of your ground, until you are destroyed; it also shall not leave you grain, wine, or oil, the increase of your herds or the young of your flock, until they have caused you to perish.

52 "They shall besiege you in all your towns, until your high and fortified walls, in which you trusted, come down throughout all your land. And they shall besiege you in all your towns throughout all your land, which the LORD your God has given you. 53 And you shall eat the fruit of your womb, the flesh of your sons and daughters, whom the LORD your God has given you, in the siege and in the distress with which your enemies shall distress you. 54 The man who is the most tender and refined among you will begrudge food to his brother, to the wife he embraces, and to the last of the children whom he has left, 55 so that he will not give to any of them any of the flesh of his children whom he is eating, because he has nothing else left, in the siege and in the distress with which your enemy shall distress you in all your towns. 56 The most tender and refined woman among you, who

would not venture to set the sole of her foot on the ground because she is so delicate and tender, will begrudge to the husband she embraces, to her son and to her daughter, 57 her afterbirth that comes out from between her feet and her children whom she bears, because lacking everything she will eat them secretly, in the siege and in the distress with which your enemy shall distress you in your towns.

58 "If you are not careful to do all the words of this law that are written in this book, that you may fear this glorious and awesome name, the LORD your God, 59 then the LORD will bring on you and your offspring extraordinary afflictions, afflictions severe and lasting, and sicknesses grievous and lasting. 60 And he will bring upon you again all the diseases of Egypt, of which you were afraid, and they shall cling to you. 61 Every sickness also and every affliction that is not recorded in the book of this law, the LORD will bring upon you, until you are destroyed. 62 Whereas you were as numerous as the stars of heaven, you shall be left few in number, because you did not obey the voice of the LORD your God. 63 And as the LORD took delight in doing you good and multiplying you, so the

LORD will take delight in bringing ruin upon you and destroying you. And you shall be plucked off the land that you are entering to take possession of it.

64 "And the LORD will scatter you among all peoples, from one end of the earth to the other, and there you shall serve other gods of wood and stone, which neither you nor your fathers have known. 65 And among these nations you shall find no respite, and there shall be no resting place for the sole of your foot, but the LORD will give you there a trembling heart and failing eyes and a languishing soul. 66 Your life shall hang in doubt before you. Night and day you shall be in dread and have no assurance of your life. 67 In the morning you shall say, 'If only it were evening!' and at evening you shall say, 'If only it were morning!' because of the dread that your heart shall feel, and the sights that your eyes shall see. 68 And the LORD will bring you back in ships to Egypt, a journey that I promised that you should never make again; and there you shall offer yourselves for sale to your enemies as male and female slaves, but there will be no buyer."

Wow! Talk about *thlipsis*; talk about oppression, suffering, persecution and affliction. Talk about tribulation! If the nation of Israel would only be faithful to God, all kinds of amazing blessings would befall her (see the first 14 verses of Deuteronomy 28). But if she rejected her Lord, if she turned from his ways, tribulation would be the inevitable outcome.

The Great Tribulation

We are now going to jump into a verse-by-verse study of Matthew 24. But before we do, let's look at one verse in the middle of the chapter (and one more verse in Revelation 1). In verse 21, Jesus said, "For then there will be *great tribulation*, such as has not been from the beginning of the world until now, no, and never will be." This is where the phrase comes from—"The Great Tribulation." Whatever Jesus is speaking of in this chapter, people have titled it "The Great Tribulation" based on this verse. I intend to show that this Great Tribulation was something that happened to the people of Israel after they rejected and crucified their God, and after they went on a wholesale attack to eradicate the followers of Jesus. I suggest to you that Matthew 24 is a confirmation of Deuteronomy 28, and that it was fulfilled in the years leading up to A.D. 70, when the Roman armies came in and leveled Jerusalem, destroyed the Temple and murdered hundreds of thousands of Jews.

Just one more verse before we get serious with our study of Matthew 24. In Revelation 1.9 John wrote, "I, John, your brother and partner in the tribulation and the kingdom and the patient endurance that are in Jesus, was on the island called Patmos on account of the word of God and the testimony of Jesus." Did you notice it? John wrote to the churches in Asia Minor (the churches under his apostolic and episcopal care) and said that he was their partner "*in the tribulation.*" Not just "tribulation"—troubles, hard times—but *the* tribulation: *te thlipsis.* What the book of the Revelation of Jesus Christ describes is the same thing that Matthew 24 describes, and, for John (not for us) it was a present-tense reality.

Now, let's dig in.

When Will This Happen?

"Jesus left the temple and was going away, when his disciples came to point out to him the buildings of the temple. But he answered them,

45

'You see all these, do you not? Truly, I say to you, there will not be left here one stone upon another that will not be thrown down.' As he sat on the Mount of Olives, the disciples came to him privately, saying, 'Tell us, when will these things be, and what will be the sign of your coming and of the end of the age?'" (Matthew 24.1-3).

What Jesus said to the disciples was earthshaking. The Temple would be destroyed. We can't even begin to imagine the impact of such a statement. It would be like him telling a Roman Catholic, "St. Peter's Basilica is going to be wiped out." It would be like him telling an American, "Washington D.C., with all its national monuments and historic buildings, is going to be obliterated." Such a thing simply wasn't on their radar at all. It was unimaginable. It was *bigger* than the Vatican and D.C. being wiped out, because the Temple stood for God's presence with his people. It was their source of spiritual identity. It was where the sacrifices occurred and prayer happened. It was the center of their universe, and the direction they knelt toward and prayed, wherever in the world they might find themselves. It was the epicenter of their national *and* spiritual identity. For it to fall, in their minds, meant *the end of their world.*

So the disciples asked him when it was going to happen: "Tell us, when will these things be, and what will be the sign of your coming and of the end of the age?"

The End of the Age

We read the verse, and notice the words, "the end of the age," and assume it's talking about the end of everything. But notice how this phrase is used in Scripture.

In 1 Corinthians 10, Paul describes for his readers the awful things that happened to the people of Israel when they got caught up in idolatry. He warns the first century Christians to not make the same mistake, and then he says, "Now these things happened to them as an example, but they were written down for *our* instruction, *on whom the end of the ages has come*" (v. 11). Notice—for Paul, the end of the ages wasn't sometime in the far off future (like, say, 2012 or later), but in the here-and-now. Paul affirms that he and the Corinthian Christians were already living in "the end of the ages."

The writer of Hebrews says it even more clearly. He describes Jesus ascending to the Father, there to make intercession for us.

He did this, Hebrews tells us, after he had offered himself once and for all as a sacrifice for our sins. Now, before we read the text, let me ask you a question: When did Jesus offer himself, once and for all, as a sacrifice to do away with our sins? Of course the answer is, on the cross. Notice the language: "For Christ has entered, not into holy places made with hands, which are copies of the true things, but into heaven itself, now to appear in the presence of God on our behalf. Nor was it to offer himself repeatedly, as the high priest enters the holy places every year with blood not his own, for then he would have had to suffer repeatedly since the foundation of the world. But as it is, he has appeared once for all *at the end of the ages* to put away sin by the sacrifice of himself" (Hebrews 9.24-26). Christ offered himself "at the end of the ages." The writer understood that the first century— when Jesus died, rose again, ascended, sent the Holy Spirit and sent the Church out on mission—was "the end of the ages."

Maybe these writers were wrong. But if they were wrong about this, maybe they were wrong about everything else they said. Maybe they were right, and our popular understanding has been wrong. "The end of the ages" was the beginning of a new era—the era of the New Covenant. All the ages past simply fell to the Lordship of Christ. From a Christian perspective, the age of the Old Testament Law (and for that matter, the ages of the Babylonian, Persian, Greek and Roman Empires) crumbled before the Lord of History who was inaugurating his Kingdom and his rule and his age. In New Testament thinking, there is simply this: the past ages, and the age of Christ.

The Last Days

Another biblical phrase that throws the modern reader for a loop is "the last days." It gets used a lot in the Bible, and modern Christians who have schooled themselves with popular novels and sensational books think "the last days" refers to the end of history. Once again, let's see how the Bible itself interprets the phrase.

When the writer of Hebrews describes the time of Jesus' coming in the flesh (remember, we're talking about a date of about 4 B.C.), he says, "Long ago, at many times and in many ways, God spoke to our fathers by the prophets, but *in these last days* he has spoken to us by his Son, whom he appointed the heir of all things, through whom also he created the world. He is the radiance of the glory of God and the exact imprint of his nature, and he upholds the universe by the word of his power. After making purification for sins, he sat down at the right hand of the Majesty on high, having become as much superior to angels as the name he has inherited is more excellent than theirs" (Hebrews 1.1-4).

When, I ask you, did God speak to us by his Son? When did his Son make purification for our sins? When did his Son sit down at the right hand of the Majesty on high? We know the dates! 4 B.C., A.D. 30, the birth, death, and resurrection of Jesus — "the last days."

There is more — much more (and we will get to it shortly), but let us pause and ask, "The last days of *what*?" Certainly not the last days of the world, not the last days of history. What the writers are speaking of here is the last days of "the ages" — the last days of everything before Christ. *The last days of the Old Covenant!* The Old Covenant began, some say, with Adam, or with Abraham, but without question it was codified and established with Moses. Jesus came as one "born under the Law," "in the fullness of time" (Galatians 4.4), but he came to fulfill the Law and abolish its tyranny.

So, the *last days* of the Old Covenant are the *first days* of the New Covenant. To be even more specific, ***the "last days" are the forty year period between the death of Christ (when the New Covenant was established) and the destruction of the Temple (when the Old Covenant, with its sacrifices and offerings, was brought to an end).*** (*This may be the most important sentence in the chapter, so mark it well*). In other words, the last days are from A.D. 30 to A.D. 70. There is a forty-year overlap of the two covenants. Jesus died on the cross and instituted the New Covenant, but the Old Covenant continued throughout the lives of most of the Apostles (only St. John outlived "the last days"). For forty years the Gospel was going forward, all across Israel and into the nations, and at the same time sacrifices were being offered in the Temple—sacrifices which were abominable—how could the sacrifice of a dove or a goat or a bull have any merit in light of the sacrifice of the Son of God?

Now, back to the Scriptures.

In 1 Timothy, Paul writes his young understudy, and warns him, "Now the Spirit expressly says that in *later times* some will depart from the faith by devoting themselves to deceitful spirits and teachings of demons" (1

Timothy 4.1). If you read it in context, he is speaking of the very days in which Timothy lives, and he goes on to say, "have nothing to do with irreverent, silly myths" (v. 7).

In his next letter to Timothy, he expands upon the theme: "But understand this, that in the *last days* there will come times of difficulty. For people will be lovers of self, lovers of money, proud, arrogant, abusive, disobedient to their parents, ungrateful, unholy, heartless, unappeasable, slanderous, without self-control, brutal, not loving good, treacherous, reckless, swollen with conceit, lovers of pleasure rather than lovers of God, having the appearance of godliness, but denying its power" (2 Timothy 3.1-5).

How many times have we heard sermons telling us that this is what we have to look forward to? That, however hard the Church strives, it is inevitable that the world will go to hell in a handbasket. We have been taught that this is a description of *our* future. But note how Paul ends verse 5: "Avoid such people." He is saying, "Timothy—in the last days people are going to be worthless, evil, and really jerks. But Timothy, you stay away from these people!" How, I ask you, could Timothy stay away from these "last days people" unless he was living in the last days?

Not, remember, the last days of the world, but the last days of the Old Covenant, that overlapping 40 years when the two covenants existed side by side.

Onward we go! And we switch now from Paul to John (could they both have been wrong-headed in what they wrote under the inspiration of the Holy Spirit?). As I mentioned earlier, John is the only Apostle who outlived the Old Covenant. Israel was destroyed in A.D. 70. By then, all the Apostles had been martyred except John. Not that they didn't try to kill him, but he survived. Shortly before the destruction of Jerusalem, John was exiled to the Isle of Patmos where received his Revelation of Jesus Christ. As a long-liver who had seen his brothers murdered one after the other, as a pastor who had watched his flocks being torn apart and persecuted, as a prophet who knew that he was smack-dab in the middle of the last days—no, even at the end of the last days, he wrote, "Children, it is *the last hour*, and as you have heard that antichrist is coming, so now many antichrists have come. Therefore we know that it is *the last hour*" (1 John 2.18). As John was writing this epistle, he clearly understood that it wasn't only the last days, it was the last hour! And, by the way, he understood that antichrist (that is, not just one, but many antichrist*s*) had already come.

The book of Revelation fits precisely into this time frame as well. John, from Patmos, is not writing about things in the far off future. He is writing about things coming down the pike immediately. Note the context in which he sets his Revelation: "The revelation of Jesus Christ, which God gave him to show to his servants the things that *must soon take place*. He made it known by sending his angel to his servant John, who bore witness to the word of God and to the testimony of Jesus Christ, even to all that he saw. Blessed is the one who reads aloud the words of this prophecy, and blessed are those who hear, and who keep what is written in it, for *the time is near*" (Revelation 1.1-3).

John wasn't writing about the 21st century or later. *Twice* in the first three verses of the book, he sets the time frame: "must soon take place," and "the time is near." Was John wrong? Was Paul wrong? Or have we been wrong? I would suggest that the book of Revelation finds its prophetic place alongside the teachings of Jesus, Paul's writings, and Peter's writings. John was referring to the Great Tribulation that was about to unfold before his very eyes, indeed, in which he was a sufferer (remember, Revelation 1.9: "I, John, your brother and partner in the tribulation...").

Finally, not only does the Revelation begin by establishing the timeframe of soon, it ends the same way. "And he said to me, 'Do not seal up the words of the prophecy of this book, for *the time is near*'" (Revelation 22.10).

All the biblical writers understood that they themselves were living in the last days. They were not giving warnings for people two millennia down the road (and skipping over more than 2000 years worth of church history —how arrogant our generation has been to assume that these things were written just for us!). They were writing pastoral letters and prophecies and revelations from God about what was happening *in their own day*. The last days. Of the Old Covenant.

Chapter Three
Wars And Rumors of Wars

I was born in 1959, so the first war I remember was Vietnam. Since then there have been a handful of military conflicts in which the United States has been involved, but, beginning with Vietnam, and moving right on through to the present day conflicts in Iraq and Afghanistan, I have heard it proclaimed from pulpit, radio and television that these are "signs of the times" because in the last days, there will be "wars and rumors of wars." Surely, the unsettled condition of bellicose nations is a sign of the soon coming of Jesus.

Never mind that, as wars go, our own time is much better than ages past. Working backwards from as little as 60 years ago: World War II saw 25 million soldiers die, with a total death count closer to 75 million (this is the largest loss of life in any war in history in actual number, but not in percentage of living population; stunningly, this number represents about 3% of the world population—but the Mongol Invasion of the 13th through 15th centuries killed an unimaginable 17% of the world population!). The American Civil War's deadliest single day took place at Antietam, with 23,000 casualties. But this battle pales in comparison to the Battle of Leipzig (in what is now Germany) when, over the course of three days in 1813, there were over 124,000 casualties. I could go on with long lists of battles and wars that make our late 20th and early 21st century wars look like child's play. But let me mention just two more: the Battle of Plataea, in Greece, in 479 B.C., which saw, according to Herodotus writing 40 years later, a death count of 257,000. And then this one, which is pertinent to our discussion: the siege of Jerusalem, in A.D. 70, when, according to the eyewitness historian Josephus, 1.1 million Jews died at the hands of the Romans.

I have actually had well-meaning Christians tell me how concerned they were for children being born into our world at our time, because, you know, "things are getting worse and worse." My response has been an incredulous, "What are you *talking* about?" On any count—war, medicine, education, technology, freedom, longevity, you name it—

the world as a whole is much better off than the world as a whole has ever been before.

But back to the subject at hand, people saying that the modern day newscasts are "proof positive" that we're living in the last days. The Bible promises wars before the return of Christ, we are told. But, at the same time, we need to pray for peace. Nevertheless, even though we might pray for peace (the Bible commands us to: "Pray for the peace of Jerusalem" [Psalm 122.6], "First of all, then, I urge that supplications, prayers, intercessions, and thanksgivings be made for all people, for kings and all who are in high positions, that we may lead a peaceful and quiet life, godly and dignified in every way" [1 Timothy 2.1,2]), we shouldn't actually expect our prayers to be answered—certainly not in any kind of definitive way.

So, we pray for peace, but Scripture also teaches us to pray for the coming of the Lord ("Our Lord, come!" [1 Corinthians 16.22]). Early on I was troubled by this seeming contradiction. On the one hand, I was commanded to pray for peace, and on the other hand I was directed to pray for the coming of the Lord. But, the coming of the Lord necessitated wars and rumors of wars. Weren't my prayers canceling each other out?

Steven Wright, the master of one-line comedy, once said that he bought a vaporizer and a dehumidifier and turned them both on in the same room, just to watch them duke it out. That's what I felt my prayers were doing—duking it out.

Then I understood that Matthew 24 and the whole "wars and rumors of war" thing wasn't about the end of time, but the end of the Old Covenant age. Let's look at the text.

"And Jesus answered them, 'See that no one leads you astray. For many will come in my name, saying, "I am the Christ," and they will lead many astray. And you will hear of wars and rumors of wars. See that you are not alarmed, for this must take place, but the end is not yet. For nation will rise against nation, and kingdom against kingdom, and there will be famines and earthquakes in various places. All these are but the beginning of the birth pains.

"'Then they will deliver you up to tribulation and put you to death, and you will be hated by all nations for my name's sake. And then many will fall away and betray one another and hate one another. And many false prophets will arise and lead many astray. And because lawlessness will be increased, the love of many

will grow cold. But the one who endures to the end will be saved'" (Matthew 24.4-13).

In this section, Jesus tells his disciples that before the end of the age (the Old Covenant age) several things will happen. There will be false prophets and false messiahs, there will be wars among the nations, there will be famines and earthquakes, and there will be persecution of Christians. Now, let's take a look at what the Apostles wrote about these things happening *in their own time.*

False Prophets

John, writing toward the end of the Old Covenant era (only a few years before A.D. 70) writes, "Beloved, do not believe every spirit, but test the spirits to see whether they are from God, for *many false prophets have gone out into the world*" (1 John 4.1). Of course, John lived to see the fulfillment of Jesus' words. He lived to see the tail end of the Old Covenant. But before him, in the book of Acts, we see these false teachers and prophets already emerging: "When they had gone through the whole island as far as Paphos, they came upon a certain magician, *a Jewish false prophet* named Bar-Jesus" (Acts. 13.6). When Paul was saying goodbye to his beloved church in Ephesus, he was grieved because, he said, "I know that after my departure *fierce wolves will come in among you,* not sparing the flock." A good portion of Paul's writings were written specifically to combat false teaching that had crept into the Church—especially the book of Galatians, which confronts the vicious wolves of legalism, parading as Christian sheep.

When giving advice to his understudies, he wrote to Titus, "For *there are many* who are insubordinate, *empty talkers and deceivers,* especially those of the circumcision party. They must be silenced, since they are upsetting whole families by teaching for shameful gain what they ought not to teach" (Titus 1.10,11); and to Timothy, "Indeed, all who desire to live a godly life in Christ Jesus will be persecuted, *while evil people and impostors will go on from bad to worse, deceiving and being deceived.* But as for you, continue in what you have learned and have firmly believed, knowing from whom you learned it" (2 Timothy 3.12-14).

Peter weighs in on the matter in his second epistle: "But false prophets also arose among the people, *just as there will be false teachers among you*, who will *secretly bring in destructive heresies*, even denying the Master who bought them, bringing upon themselves swift destruction. And many will follow their sensuality, and because of them the way of truth will be blasphemed. And in their greed they will exploit you with false words. Their condemnation from long ago is not idle, and their destruction is not asleep" (2 Peter 2.1-3). In fact, Second Peter and Jude are written specifically to counter false prophets and teachers during the time of the Apostles.

This is to not even take into consideration the many false prophets and false teachers not mentioned in the Bible but recorded in history. Josephus tells the stories of no less than thirteen men stating messianic claims, in the first century alone.

Wars And Rumors Of Wars

Jesus and the Apostles lived during the rule of the Roman Empire. In trying to enforce the *Pax Romana* (the "Peace of Rome"), the Empire found itself constantly trying to squash rebellions, including the British rebellion, three Jewish rebellions, a German rebellion and a Balkan rebellion, not to mention a Roman civil war in which three

Caesars were assassinated within one year (Galba, Otho, and Vitellius) — the year, coincidentally, was A.D. 69. Certainly, during the last days of the Old Covenant, there was constant discussion about the wars, and the saber rattling, going on in the Empire. And as the end approached, those rumors became reality as the mighty machinery of Rome turned toward Jerusalem herself, laying siege to her for three and a half years before crushing her into the ground.

Famines

In the book of Acts we read about a famine in Jerusalem that hurt the Christians there in a bad way. "Now in these days prophets came down from Jerusalem to Antioch. And one of them named Agabus stood up and foretold by the Spirit that there would be a great famine over all the world (this took place in the days of Claudius). So the disciples determined, every one according to his ability, to send relief to the brothers living in Judea. And they did so, sending it to the elders by the hand of Barnabas and Saul" (Acts. 11.27-30). Later, as Paul made his missionary journeys, he was faithful to take up special offerings for the suffering back in Jerusalem.

True to the prophetic word, during the reign of the Emperor Claudius (A.D. 41-54)) several severe famines struck the Roman World. These famines were caused by lack of rainfall, blasting hot winds, destructive plagues of locusts, and even untimely frosts. Of course, wars themselves brought famines, destroying farmlands and disrupting the lives of farmers, many called into battle. Syria saw a famine so severe that hundreds of thousands starved to death. Around the year 47 famine struck Jerusalem, and it was somewhat allayed by grain sent from Egypt. And in Rome itself, the hungry people revolted against Claudius, attacking him personally. Ironically, Claudius died, not from a lack of food, but from eating food—which had been poisoned by his wife, so her son, Nero, could assume the throne.

Earthquakes

They aren't anything new. Earthquakes have been happening, well, since the earth was formed. A great earthquake destroyed Pompeii and the Bay of Naples in A.D. 62. Acts 16.26 records a "violent earthquake" which shook Philippi and freed Paul and Silas from their chains. Asia Minor (modern

Turkey) was, and still is, a center for significant earthquake activity, and experienced major earthquakes during the Apostolic era. The Stoic philosopher Seneca wrote in one of his letters, "How often have cities in Asia, how often has Achaia, been laid low by a single shock of earthquake! How many towns in Smyrna, how many in Macedonia, have been swallowed up! How often has Paphos collapsed! Not infrequently are tidings brought to us of the utter destruction of entire cities."[1]

When Jesus warned the Apostles about the coming earthquakes, they weren't portents of the end of the world, they were things which had been happening forever, and they would continue to happen as the end of the age approached.

Persecutions

Only a few modern Christians in the Western World have experienced real persecution. In the state of Chiapas, Mexico, in the last 30 years, families who converted to

---

[1] Seneca; *Ad Lucillum Epistulae Morales*; Translation by Richard M. Gummere; London, Heinemann; 1917; Volume 2, Page 437.

Christianity have had their homes burned and been driven out of town. This is persecution. In various places in Africa, Muslims who convert to Christianity are beheaded. This is real persecution. In China, people who convert to Christianity are sometimes imprisoned. This is real persecution. People making fun of your religion isn't persecution.

Just like earthquakes, persecution isn't anything new. Ten of the eleven disciples (I'm not counting Judas here) were tortured and murdered for their faith. John was exiled to a rock island. The book of Acts contains a virtual litany of persecutions against the early church, with all the chief players being imprisoned, tortured, or killed for their faith: Stephen, Barnabas, Silas, Peter, John, James, and others. Paul himself was a persecutor of the church who was later converted and himself died at the hands of persecutors. Luke recounts Paul's role in Acts 8: "And Saul approved of his execution. And there arose on that day a great persecution against the church in Jerusalem, and they were all scattered throughout the regions of Judea and Samaria, except the apostles. Devout men buried Stephen and made great lamentation over him. But Saul was ravaging the church, and entering house after house, he dragged off men and women and committed them to prison" (Acts 8.1-3).

After the initial wave of persecution, which caused a scattering of the Jerusalem church, we read of yet another one: "About that time Herod the king laid violent hands on some who belonged to the church" (Acts 12.1). It was during this persecution that James was murdered and Peter was imprisoned.

As the Apostles went beyond Jerusalem with the Gospel—all throughout the Roman Empire—they were persecuted wherever they went. After a successful campaign in Antioch Pisidia, we read, "But the Jews incited the devout women of high standing and the leading men of the city, stirred up persecution against Paul and Barnabas, and drove them out of their district" (Acts. 13.50).

Paul warned believers in Thessalonica that persecution would be part of their lives as they followed after Jesus: "For you, brothers, became imitators of the churches of God in Christ Jesus that are in Judea. For you suffered the same things from your own countrymen as they did from the Jews, who killed both the Lord Jesus and the prophets, and drove us out, and displease God and oppose all mankind by hindering us from speaking to the Gentiles that they might be saved—so as always to fill up the measure of their sins. But wrath has come upon them at last" (1 Thessalonians 2.14-16). Later in the same epistle, Paul wrote, "and we sent Timothy, our brother and God's coworker in the gospel of Christ, to establish and exhort you in your faith, that no one be moved by these afflictions. For you yourselves know that we are destined for this. For when we were with you, we kept telling you beforehand that we were to suffer affliction, just as it has come to pass, and just as you know" (3.2-4).

Finally, the writer of Hebrews recounts what the early Christians had to endure: "But recall the former days when, after you were enlightened, you endured a hard struggle with sufferings, sometimes being publicly exposed to reproach and affliction, and sometimes being partners with those so treated. For you had compassion on those in prison, and you joyfully accepted the plundering of your property, since you knew that you yourselves had a better possession and an abiding one" (Hebrews 10.32-34).

The point? Persecution isn't a mark of the end of history, a precedent for the Second Coming; persecution is a mark of the end of the Old Covenant age, and something the early church endured with joy and hope.

Apostasy

Among the preachers and teachers I encountered in my earlier life, there was always much talk about "the great falling away." We were taught to expect a massive, wholesale abandonment of the faith, with only a remnant remaining faithful. Depending on which legalistic circle one moved in, this abandonment of the faith might be signified by so-called Christians starting to go to movies or starting to dance. Certainly those who worshiped liturgically had abandoned the faith, "having a *form* of godliness, but denying the power thereof," we were told, being quoted the King James Version of 2 Timothy 3.5 — a passage detailing what would happen "in the last days." "Sipping-saints?" Forget about it; these people were the epitome of the great falling away. Not to mention the real quacks who had abandoned the faith (if they had ever had possession of it to begin with) — David Koresh (formerly 7th Day Adventist), Jim Jones (formerly Assemblies of God), and John Shelby Spong (still an Episcopalian). All these, we understood, were indicators of the soon coming of Christ; they were proof that the apostasy predicted by Jesus in Matthew 24 was barreling full speed toward us.

But of course, by now you know, the evidence is in that apostasy was a first century reality. Jesus wasn't talking about the 20th or 21st century or beyond. He was talking about a real apostasy that would occur within the lives of the Apostles — in the last days of the Old Covenant.

Much of Paul's writing was to battle against the false teachers who were leading astray many and causing them to abandon the faith. He writes to the church in Galatia, "O foolish Galatians! Who has bewitched you? It was before your eyes that Jesus Christ was publicly portrayed as crucified. Let me ask you only this: Did you receive the Spirit by works of the law or by hearing with faith? Are you so foolish? Having begun by the Spirit, are you now being perfected by the flesh?" (Galatians 3.1-3).

In Acts, Paul warns the Christians in Ephesus, "from among your own selves will arise men speaking twisted things, to draw away the disciples after them" (Acts 20.30).

Once again, the last Apostle gets the last word. After all the others had died at the hands of persecutors, John writes, "Children, it is the last hour, and as you have heard that antichrist is coming, so now many antichrists have come. Therefore we know that it is the last hour. They went out from us, but they were not of us; for if they had been of us, they would have continued with us. But they went out, that it might become plain that they all are not of us" (1 John 2.18-19). Old John understood the times. It was not only the last days, it was the last hour. Antichrists were afoot, apostasy was in process. Times were tough. A Great Tribulation was near. Matthew 24 wasn't knocking at the door, it had knocked the door clean away and had stomped into the room.

Chapter Three
Then The End Will Come

Picture a seed pod with precious, valuable seeds inside it. Now, understand that the pod, for whatever reason, has to be destroyed. But the seeds are important. They have to be saved. So before the pod can be destroyed, the seeds have to be disbursed.

Now, picture the city of Jerusalem. The first mention we find of the place is all the way back in Genesis, when it was the domain of a mysterious priest/king who was a "priest of the most high God," Melchizedek. Abraham, who is from the land of Ur, and from a family of Moon-worshipers, is called by God to leave his people and journey to a promised land. When he arrives, he encounters this mysterious priest (who, according to the book of Hebrews, is a kind of antetype of Christ himself). After Abraham is victorious in a great battle, he approaches Melchizedek, who brings out bread and wine, and blesses Abraham. In response, Abraham gives him a tithe of all his winnings (this is the first time tithing is mentioned in the Bible, and it happens 430 years before the giving of the Law to Moses—but that is for another discussion). You can read the whole story in Genesis 14, but isn't it interesting that to this day, in the Christian Church, the priests of Christ (who are in the line of Melchizedek because Jesus himself was in the line of Melchizedek—read the whole of Hebrews 6 and 7) bring out bread and wine and bless the people, and the people tithe to the priesthood? But I digress—we're talking about Jerusalem. Jerusalem is where Melchizedek reigned, and from that time forward it is recognized as the favorite city of God, "beautiful for situation, the joy of the whole earth" (Psalm 48.2, KJV).

Later, King David captures it and it is called "The City of David." David's son, Solomon, builds a Temple there; the Ark of the Presence is relocated to the Holy of Holies in the Temple and the glory of God inhabits it. His presence is so strong that the priests can't perform their liturgy. After that Temple falls, the prophets promise an even greater Temple will be built—not because it is grander in style or size, but because a greater glory of God will fill it.

It is in this Temple that Jesus sits as a twelve year old boy, stumping the teachers of the Law. It is in this Temple that Jesus teaches. It is in this Temple that Jesus walks through the courtyard, making a whip from the leather thongs of the cages as he releases the animals, and clears the Temple of the ungodly commerce going on in its hallowed halls. And it is this City of God and this Temple which Jesus tells his disciples will come tumbling down.

But wait! It can't come tumbling down —not *yet*! Why, this is the Temple and the City which houses the New Covenant. This is the place where the only Christians in the whole world live and worship. Acts tells us, about the early Christians, "And day by day, attending the temple together and breaking bread in their homes, they received their food with glad and generous hearts" (Acts 2.46). How could God destroy this Temple, this city? Doesn't he know that if he destroys it, he destroys the New Covenant which it houses? Of course he knows.

So Jesus told the disciples, as his last bit of instruction before he ascended to the Father, "go into all the world" (Matthew 28.19). "He ordered them not to depart from Jerusalem, but to wait for the promise of the Father, which, he said, 'you heard from me; for John baptized with water, but you will be baptized with the Holy Spirit not many days from now...But you will receive power when the Holy Spirit has come upon you, and you will be my witnesses in Jerusalem and in all Judea and Samaria, and to the end of the earth'" (Acts 1.4-8).

Here was the problem: The New Covenant was localized in Jerusalem, but Jerusalem was about to be destroyed. Before the "pod" of Jerusalem could be destroyed, the "seeds" of the Gospel had to get outside its walls.

Here was the solution: whatever it takes, get the Gospel outside the walls of Jerusalem. It happened in a couple of ways. First, the Day of Pentecost came when the Holy Spirit fell on the disciples, and Jews from all over the world heard the Good News of Jesus. In one day 3000 believed and were baptized. How's that for effective evangelism? These folk went back to their foreign countries, having been born again, having received the gift of the Holy Spirit, and carrying with them the Gospel of Jesus.

Shortly after this initial dispersion, there occurred a dispersion by persecution. The book of Acts records (as we have already learned) that a great persecution arose in Jerusalem against the Christians, and that they fled. After the martyrdom of the Apostle James, all the Apostles left town. In this way places as far off as India received the Gospel (the early church father and historian Eusebius tells us that the Apostle Bartholomew went to India, and took with him a Hebrew version of the Gospel of Matthew!). John went to Asia Minor, Peter went to Asia Minor and then to Rome, Mark went to Egypt, and Paul, the late-comer, went all over the place—Asia Minor, Crete, Cyprus, Greece, Rome and even as far as Spain (and some would argue possibly Britain, a Roman colony at the time). The only leader left in Jerusalem was Bishop James, the brother of Jesus, and he wrote a pastor's manual, known as the Epistle of James, to help the pastors under his care who had been scattered abroad. He begins his manual with these words: "James, a servant of God and of the Lord Jesus Christ, To the twelve tribes in the Dispersion: Greetings. Count it all joy, my brothers, when you meet trials of various kinds, for you know that the testing of your faith produces steadfastness" (James 1.1-3).

What, you may ask, has any of this to do with Matthew 24? It has everything to do with a single verse which has been completely misread and stuck at the end of world history. Verse 14:

And this gospel of the kingdom will be proclaimed throughout the whole world as a testimony to all nations, and then the end will come.

Jesus has just warned about wars, famines, earthquakes — "but the end is not yet." He tells the disciples they will be persecuted, and false prophets will arise, and the love of many will grow cold, but *still* the end is not yet! "Well, then, when *is* the end of the Old Covenant?" they might well ask. "Ah!" Jesus would respond, "I'm glad you asked. Before the Old Covenant, along with the Temple and the City of Jerusalem, is brought to an end, this Gospel of the New Covenant, the Gospel of the Kingdom, has to be proclaimed in the whole world." Before the pod is destroyed, the seeds have to be dispersed.

And that is exactly what happened. Before Jerusalem was laid waste by the invading Roman armies in A.D. 70, the Gospel of Jesus Christ was taken... *"throughout the world"!*

It is at this point that my popular-theology-friends raise their first red flag (I promise, they will raise more red flags before we're done here). "Seriously? You expect me to believe that before A.D. 70 the Gospel had made it 'throughout the world'?" And my response is, "Don't take my word for it. Read it for yourself."

First, the Day of Pentecost: "Now there were dwelling in Jerusalem Jews, devout men *from every nation under heaven.* And at this sound the multitude came together, and they were bewildered, because each one was hearing them speak in his own language. And they were amazed and astonished, saying, 'Are not all these who are speaking Galileans? And how is it that we hear, each of us in his own native language? Parthians and Medes and Elamites and residents of Mesopotamia, Judea and Cappadocia, Pontus and Asia, Phrygia and Pamphylia, Egypt and the parts of Libya belonging to Cyrene, and visitors from Rome, both Jews and proselytes, Cretans and Arabians—we hear them telling in our own tongues the mighty works of God'" (Acts 2.5-11).

It was this group of Pentecost believers, "from every nation under heaven," who went back to their homes as the first international evangelists, carrying the Good News of Jesus with them, sharing it with their families and friends.

Later in Acts we read of Paul preaching in Antioch (in Asia Minor), "The next Sabbath almost the whole city gathered to hear the word of the Lord. But when the Jews saw the crowds, they were filled with jealousy and began to contradict what was spoken by Paul, reviling him. And Paul and Barnabas spoke out boldly, saying, 'It was necessary that the word of God be spoken first to you. Since you thrust it aside and judge yourselves unworthy of eternal life, behold, we are turning to the Gentiles. For so the Lord has commanded us, saying, "I have made you a light for the Gentiles, *that you may bring salvation to the ends of the earth*"'" (Acts 13.44-47).

Paul and Barnabas understood their call—to take the Good News of salvation "to the ends of the earth." And they did just that. In Romans, Paul confirms what he said in Acts: "For there is no distinction between Jew and Greek; for the same Lord is Lord of all, bestowing his riches on all who call on him. For 'everyone who calls on the name of the Lord will be saved.' How then will they call on him in whom they have not believed? And how are they to believe in him of whom they have never heard? And how are they to hear without someone preaching? And how are they to preach unless they are sent? As it is written, 'How beautiful are the feet of those who preach the good news!' But they have not all obeyed the gospel. For Isaiah says, 'Lord, who has believed what he has heard from us?' So faith comes from hearing, and hearing through the word of Christ. But I ask, have they not heard? Indeed they have, [*then, quoting Psalm 19.4*] for '*Their voice has gone out to all the earth, and their words to the ends of the world.*'"

Not yet convinced? OK, three more passages:

Romans 16.25-27: "Now to him who is able to strengthen you according to my gospel and the preaching of Jesus Christ, according to the revelation of the mystery that was kept secret for long ages but has now been disclosed and through the prophetic writings *has been made known to all nations*, according to the command of the eternal God, to bring about the obedience of faith — to the only wise

God be glory forevermore through Jesus Christ! Amen."

Colossians 1.5, 21-23: "Of this you have heard before in the word of truth, the gospel, which has come to you, *as indeed in the whole world it is bearing fruit and increasing* —as it also does among you, since the day you heard it and understood the grace of God in truth...And you, who once were alienated and hostile in mind, doing evil deeds, he has now reconciled in his body of flesh by his death, in order to present you holy and blameless and above reproach before him, if indeed you continue in the faith, stable and steadfast, not shifting from the hope of the gospel that you heard, *which has been proclaimed in all creation under heaven*, and of which I, Paul, became a minister."

1 Timothy 3.16: "Great indeed, we confess, is the mystery of godliness: He was manifested in the flesh, vindicated by the Spirit, seen by angels, *proclaimed among the nations, believed on in the world*, taken up in glory."

In Matthew 24, Jesus said the end (of the Old Covenant, of the Temple, of Jerusalem) could not happen until the Gospel of the Kingdom was proclaimed throughout the whole world. It was.

Chapter Five
The Abomination of Desolation

Walt Disney helped me be a Dispensationalist. I remember visiting Disneyland when I was about 8 years old. For a Texas country boy, a trip to Anaheim, California was like a trip to the Moon, and Disneyland seemed technologically advanced beyond imagination. No, I'm not talking about the rides, or the shows; I'm talking about that amazingly lifelike, talking, moving robot of Abraham Lincoln. If you are "of a certain age," and had the privilege of visiting Disneyland during the 1960s, you will know what I'm talking about. Abraham Lincoln stood there in that auditorium, turning, looking this way and that, opening his mouth, and *talking to us*! Looking back on it with 45 years of perspective, the Abe exhibit was a little corny, and, compared to the robots of today, Honest Abe wasn't anywhere near lifelike.

A few years after my visit to Disneyland, I was told that the Abraham Lincoln moving statue was a whole lot like a statue the Antichrist would set up in the Temple, during the future Great Tribulation, which people who had received a 666 tattoo on their forehead would be forced to worship. I'm not sure now how the notion that the Abomination of Desolation was a robot-statue came about theologically, but, somehow, this all made sense to me.

What the preachers and teachers were referring to was something mentioned by Jesus in Matthew 24.15 called "The Abomination of Desolation."

> *"So when you see the abomination of desolation spoken of by the prophet Daniel, standing in the holy place (let the reader understand)..."*

Let's get this straight. The Abomination of Desolation is not a future thing, and is not a statue. "How do I know?" you ask—let me show you.

"Spoken Of By The Prophet Daniel"

Modern readers may make wild guesses as to what this abomination is, but the original readers of Matthew were more savvy and closer to the moment, and understood what Jesus was talking about. Matthew is writing in a kind of "code language" which a Roman or a Greek might not pick up on, but a Jew schooled in the Old Testament would catch immediately. Jesus says, "So when you see the abomination of desolation...*spoken of by the prophet Daniel*..." Jesus borrows a phrase straight out of the book of Daniel. It is worth looking at in a few different English translations, because it's a little complicated to translate from the Hebrew:

> Daniel 9.27, English Standard Version: "And he shall make a strong covenant with many for one week, and for half of the week he shall put an end to sacrifice and offering. And on the wing of abominations shall come one who makes desolate, until the decreed end is poured out on the desolator."

Daniel 9:27, New American Standard Bible: "And he will make a firm covenant with the many for one week, but in the middle of the week he will put a stop to sacrifice and grain offering; and on the wing of abominations *will come* one who makes desolate, even until a complete destruction, one that is decreed, is poured out on the one who makes desolate."

Daniel 9.27, King James Version: "And he shall confirm the covenant with many for one week: and in the midst of the week he shall cause the sacrifice and the oblation to cease, and for the overspreading of abominations he shall make it desolate, even until the consummation, and that determined shall be poured upon the desolate."

Another verse, a little later in Daniel, speaks of the same thing: "Forces from him shall appear and profane the temple and fortress, and shall take away the regular burnt offering. And they shall set up the abomination that makes desolate" (Daniel 11.31).

Here is what we have so far. Whoever this "he" is, he makes a covenant with Israel for "one week" or "one seven." All theologians agree these "sevens" are weeks of years. In other words, he makes a covenant with Israel for seven years. In the middle of the seven years, he puts an end to the sacrifices and offerings, and after that there is some abominable thing—some impure, detestable thing—"which shall appear and profane the temple..." and cause desolation, that is, destruction and emptiness.

The first reference for understanding this text, as a kind of "foreshadowing event" (called, in literature and theology, an antetype), is an event that happened in 168 B.C., when the Greek emperor Antiochus Epiphanes invaded Jerusalem. Antiochus Epiphanes was not his real name, by the way —his real name was Mithridates, but he took this title for himself when he was enthroned, and it means, "God made manifest." When he invaded Jerusalem he laid siege to the Temple, sacked it, and proceeded to sacrifice a pig (an unclean animal) to Zeus, on the altar of the Temple. You can read more about this story in the book of 1 Maccabees. This foreign, pagan, evil king came in, desecrated the Temple, murdered the people, and oppressed the city. He and his forces were an abomination, which caused desolation in Jerusalem.

But Antiochus Epiphanes did his deed a good 200 years *before* Jesus gave his teaching in Matthew 24. Obviously every Jew, including Jesus, would have known the tale. The incident became a symbol of destruction, of evil running roughshod over righteousness, and of the unimaginable consequences of the profane triumphing over the sacred. It was part of their history, part of their Scripture, and part of their religious celebration. The feast of Hanukkah was an annual celebration of God delivering his people from this evil oppression.

So, whatever Jesus was speaking about, it wasn't Antiochus (that had already happened), but it was *like* Antiochus. And when he said the words, "the abomination of desolation," all his hearers would instantly know his reference. And here Jesus was, *saying it was going to happen again!*

Four Gospels To Four Target Groups

One important way of understanding something in a Gospel passage is to compare it to its sister verses in the other Gospels. If you have studied in seminary or just tried to keep up with contemporary theology, you know there are all kinds of debates and arguments and "proofs" about when the four Gospels were written, and which came first, and who wrote what. Some scholar comes up with an irrefutable theory, and everyone buys into it as ironclad. Then some other scholar comes up with a completely opposite irrefutable theory, and everyone runs over to *that* side. If you hold to last year's model of thinking, beware — you will be looked at as embarrassingly passé and ignorant, rather like a country bumpkin who just rolled into town.

But the early church understood it like this: Matthew wrote first, Mark wrote second, Luke wrote third, and John wrote fourth. Conveniently, they set the order of the Gospels in the New Testament in precisely the order they were written in. Each Gospel was written (more or less at ten years apart) to a specific audience or target group, and each Gospel represents the leadership, faith and insights of one of the Apostles. Matthew, Mark and Luke are called "the Synoptic Gospels" because they look at the Gospel *synoptically*, that is, "with the same eye." John, written last, and written specifically to Christians, has a different perspective. John doesn't record Jesus' "little apocalypse" in his Gospel, but he makes up for it in spades by giving us the book of Revelation.

The Gospel According To Matthew is "James' Gospel," and was written first. The early church tells us it was originally written in Hebrew, and if it wasn't, certainly there were Hebrew copies available *very* early on. Bartholomew took one to India before A.D. 70. It was written for a Jewish target group, so you will see more references to the Old Testament in Matthew than in any of the other gospels, and you will repeatedly see the phrase, "that it might be fulfilled what was spoken by the prophet so-and-so." In our text at hand (Matthew 24.15), Jesus says, "...the abomination of desolation, *spoken of by the prophet Daniel—let the reader understand*." Matthew is speaking to a Jewish audience that knows and understands the prophet Daniel.

The Gospel According To Mark is "Peter's Gospel," and it comes second. It shows a side of Peter, by the way, that the other Gospels hesitate to reveal—a weak, flawed, and sometimes brash side. Mark was written to the Romans, who did everything quickly and directly. They took their news straight, even if it was their Good News. The word translated "immediately" or "straightway" (*eutheos*) is used 41 times in Mark! So, when Mark gives us his verse (13.14), he completely leaves out the reference to Daniel: "But when you see the abomination of desolation standing where he ought not to be (let the reader understand)..." *Important note: Mark also replaces "standing in the holy place" with "standing where he ought not to be."*

The Gospel According To Luke is "Paul's Gospel," and it comes third. Luke was a physician, a convert through Paul's ministry, a traveling companion with Paul on his missionary journeys, an historian, and a researcher. He wasn't from Israel. He wasn't an eyewitness to Jesus. He got all his information from research and interviews. Interestingly, Luke tells us more about the Blessed Virgin Mary and the birth story of Jesus than do the other Gospels, and it makes sense that Mary would grant an interview to the beloved Doctor and reveal details to him that the others weren't privy to. Luke, who also wrote the book of Acts, wrote to the Gentiles, and specifically to a particular Greek man named Theophilus.

Because he is writing with the clarity of a researcher and to an audience which doesn't have an Old Testament frame of reference, Luke's Gospel is often the most clear and easily understood. When Luke gives us Jesus' words about the "abomination of desolation," he doesn't even use the phrase: "But when you see Jerusalem surrounded by armies, then know that its desolation has come near" (Luke 21.20). Notice. Luke replaces "abomination" with "armies." He replaces "the holy place" (Matthew) or "where he ought not be" (Mark) with "Jerusalem." He keeps the word desolation.

Put the passages all together in a chart and compare them, and come up with the answer for yourself to the question of "What is the Abomination of Desolation?"

Gospel	Matthew	Mark	Luke
What?	Abomination	Abomination	Armies
Where?	Holy place	Where he ought not stand	Jerusalem
Result?	Desolation	Desolation	Desolation

What is the Abomination of Desolation? I bet by now you see it for yourself! It isn't a robot in a future Temple. It isn't a statue. It isn't anything else of the sort. It isn't even a *future anything*! The Abomination of Desolation to which Jesus refers is the pagan armies of Rome surrounding the city of Jerusalem just like the pagan armies of Greece did over 200 years before. These Roman soldiers laid siege to the city for three and a half years, starved out the people, burned down the Temple, killed over a million people, and, like evil Antiochus Epiphanes before them, offered pagan sacrifices on the holy mountain of God.

Head for the Hills!

Just one more piece of evidence that Jesus is speaking to his generation, and not ours (or any later one). In the very next verse, after describing this abomination that causes desolation, this army surrounding Jerusalem, Jesus gives his followers instruction about what to do when they see it...

> ...then let those who are in Judea flee to the mountains. Let the one who is on the housetop not go down to take what is in his house, and let the one who is in the field not turn back to take his cloak. And alas for women who are pregnant and for those who are nursing infants in those days! Pray that your flight may not be in winter or on a Sabbath (Matthew 24.16-20).

The popular dispensational (pop-dispy for short) teachers tell us the Great Tribulation is a future event, most likely soon, which will affect the entire world. But please note the localization of what Jesus is describing. First, "let those who are in Judea flee to the mountains." No instruction for those in Texas, or Venezuela, or Mexico, or Spain, or China, or Zimbabwe. Why does he single out Judea? *Because this is a Judean event*!

Next, he says, "Let the one who is on the housetop not go down to take what is in his house." Now, I ask you, when was the last time you were on your housetop? Maybe before Christmas, stringing lights? Other than that, when? How about the Swiss and their A-frame chalets—how often do they sit up on their housetops? Obviously this is referencing the typical situation of first century Israel, where the housetops served as cool places to sit in the evening. He goes on to warn, "let the one who is in the field not turn back to take his cloak." This fellow in the field—he's not out on his air-conditioned tractor guided by GPS and listening to *The Best of Bob Dylan* while he plows. He's behind a mule, or harvesting by hand. He's not a 21st century farmboy, he's a first century Jewish family man, and the scene is a typical one for the disciples to see.

Then, three more things which help establish the context of Jesus' warning: "Alas for women who are pregnant and for those who are nursing infants in those days! Pray that your flight may not be in winter or on a Sabbath." Admittedly, modern-day pregnancy is no piece of cake, but it isn't as difficult as first-century pregnancy was. If hard times hit, there were no cars, no buses, no airplanes, in which to escape. There was only the beast of burden or your own two feet. Wintertime can be nasty all over the world. In Mexico, in February, 1836, when Santa Ana was making his way north to attack the Alamo, his army camped on the south side of the Rio Grande River, and a freak snow storm came and killed nearly a thousand soldiers who froze to death that night. Winters used to be horrible to endure. But when was the last time you heard of a thousand soldiers freezing in one wintry night? Times have changed. Jesus wasn't speaking about 21st century global winter, but first century Judean winter. And as for the Sabbath—if this is a warning for 21st century Christians, why exactly do we care if it happens on Saturday? We don't even observe the Sabbath. First century Jews were forbidden by the law of the time to work on the Sabbath, or to travel more than a mile from their homes. A siege, or a final invasion, on the Sabbath, would be catastrophic.

Just to make sure you're on the same page as I am so far (that would be page 98) — what Jesus is describing in Matthew 24 is not an end-of-the-world event, it is an end-of-the-Old-Covenant-era event, "the end of the age," the "last days" of the Old Covenant. It isn't something we fretfully anticipate in the future, it is a tragedy we look back on with amazement. It happened. Just like he said it would. In his own generation.

Chapter Six
The Great Tribulation

We finally arrive at the famous phrase itself—"Great Tribulation." Jesus said,

> *"For then there will be great tribulation, such as has not been from the beginning of the world until now, no, and never will be" (Matthew 24.21).*

So *this* is what everybody has been talking about and warning about, and scaring the life out of innocent children about. In our study we have finally come to it. And for all that has been said about the phrase, we will spend only a few short paragraphs discussing it now.

We have already seen that the word "tribulation" is a translation of the Greek word *thlipsis*, which means *trouble, suffering, oppression, affliction,* and *persecution.* Jesus tells his listeners that the suffering coming upon Jerusalem will not be run-of-the-mill suffering, but *great* affliction. But please note the timeframe that Jesus gives. This is not some event that happens out toward the end of history, nor is it an even that occurs way back in earlier history. He sets the event in the middle of history—his own time—not the future, not the past, but his own *now*: "such as has not been from the beginning of the world until *now*, no, and never will be."

Some people have responded in opposition to this by saying, "Well, sure, what happened in Jerusalem in A.D. 70 was terrible, but it wasn't the greatest affliction to beset the world ever. It wasn't the *worst* tribulation to ever hit, so it can't be 'the *Great Tribulation.*' Wasn't what happened to the Jews in Nazi Germany worse than this?" This is a fair question. As far as the loss of human life, certainly, what happened in Germany was worse. But to this day the Jews mourn what happened in Jerusalem in the first century with a sense of deep grief. Tragic as the loss of human life is, what happened in Jerusalem wasn't just the loss of human life, it was the loss of *everything.* It was the loss of the Temple, God's house on the earth. It was the loss of the

Aaronic priesthood, established by God in the time of Moses. It was the loss of the sacrifices which were made for the sins of the people. It was a loss of all the rituals, all the rites, all the liturgy—it was a loss of the religion of the Jews. In fact, twenty years later, in the year 90, a group of Pharisees met in the city of Jamnia to re-invent a Judaism without a Temple (and, by the way, to toss out the Greek books of the Old Testament which the Christians were using to bolster their claims that Jesus was Messiah, books including First Maccabees, which details the previous destruction brought on by the original abomination of desolation—but that is an discussion for another day). Everything had changed. Their world had come to an end.

False Christs And Shortened Days

Continuing with his timely warnings about the soon-approaching end of the Jewish world, Jesus said,

> *"And if those days had not been cut short, no human being would be saved. But for the sake of the elect those days will be cut short. Then if anyone says to you, 'Look, here is the Christ!' or 'There he is!' do not believe it. For false christs and false prophets will arise and*

perform great signs and wonders, so as to lead astray, if possible, even the elect. See, I have told you beforehand. So, if they say to you, 'Look, he is in the wilderness,' do not go out. If they say, 'Look, he is in the inner rooms,' do not believe it. For as the lightning comes from the east and shines as far as the west, so will be the coming of the Son of Man" (Matthew 24.22-27).

My only comment on this passage is, let Josephus have a word. Josephus was a Jewish (non-Christian) historian who was an eyewitness to the destruction of Jerusalem. He wrote an amazing and thorough history of the event which merits reading by anyone seriously interested in the Great Tribulation. Here are two extensive comments by the man; it's almost like he is writing a commentary on Jesus' words.

Jesus said, "If they say to you, 'Look, he is in the wilderness,' do not go out." Josephus wrote,

Now as for the affairs of the Jews, they grew worse and worse continually; for the country was again filled with robbers and impostors who deluded the multitude...Certain of those robbers went up to the city, as if they were going to worship God, while they had daggers under their garments; and, by thus mingling themselves among the multitude, they slew Jonathan [the High Priest]; and as this murder was never avenged, the robbers went up with the greatest security at the festivals after this time...These works, that were done by the robbers, filled the city with all sorts of impiety. And now these impostors and deceivers persuaded the multitude to follow them into the wilderness, and pretended that they would exhibit manifest wonders and signs, that should be performed by the providence of God. And many that were prevailed on by them suffered the punishment of their folly; for Felix brought them back, and then punished them. Moreover, there came out of Egypt about this time to Jerusalem, one that said he was a prophet, and advised the multitude of the common people to go along with him to the Mount of Olives, as it was called, which lay over against the city, and at the distance of five furlongs. He said farther, that he would show them from hence, how, at his command, the walls of Jerusalem would fall down; and he promised them that he would procure them an entrance into the city through those walls, when they were fallen down. Now when Felix was informed of these things, he ordered his soldiers to take their weapons, and come against them with a great number of horsemen and footmen, from Jerusalem, and attacked the Egyptian and the people that were with him. He also slew four hundred of them, and took two hundred alive. But the Egyptian himself escaped out of the fight, but did not appear any more. And again the robbers stirred up the people to make war with the Romans, and said they ought not to obey them at all; and when any person would not comply with them, they set fire to their villages, and plundered them (Josephus, *Antiquities of the Jews*, Book 20, 8.5, 6).

Jesus said, "If they say, 'Look, he is in the inner rooms,' do not believe it." Josephus wrote,

And now the Romans, judging that it was in vain to spare what was round about the holy house, burnt all those places, as also the remains of the cloisters and the gates, two excepted; the one on the east side, and the one on the south: both which, however, they burnt afterward. They also burnt down the treasury chambers, in which was an immense quantity of money, and an immense number of garments, and other precious goods, there reposited; and to speak all in a few words, there it was that the entire riches of the Jews were heaped together, while the rich people had there built themselves chambers [to contain the furniture]. The soldiers came to the rest of the cloisters that were in the outer [court of the] temple, whither the women and children, and a great mixed multitude of the people fled, in number about six thousand. But before Caesar had determined anything about these people, or given the commanders any orders relating to them, the soldiers were in such a rage, that they set the cloister on fire; by which means it came to pass that some of these were destroyed by throwing themselves down headlong, and some were burnt in the cloisters themselves. Nor did any one of them escape with his life. A false prophet was the occasion of these people's destruction, who had made a public proclamation in the city that very day, that God commanded them to get up upon the temple, and that there they should receive miraculous signs of their deliverance

(Josephus; *The War of the Jews*, Volume
24, Book 6, 5.2).

Corpses and Eagles

Jesus gives a final, chilling, sentence
about this "Great Tribulation" which was to
soon befall Jerusalem:

> *"Wherever the corpse is, there the vultures will
> gather" (Matthew 24.28).*

Everyone knows what it's like to see a
bunch of buzzards or vultures flying overhead
in a circle. "Something's dead," we say. That
something, in this case, was the city of
Jerusalem. But there is more here. The Greek
word for vultures, *aetos*, is also the Greek
word for eagles. In fact, that is how the King
James version translates this passage — "For
wheresoever the carcass is, there will *the eagles*
be gathered together." It is the same word
used in Revelation to describe the heavenly
angelic creatures that John saw in his vision:
"the first living creature like a lion, the second
living creature like an ox, the third living
creature with the face of a man, and the fourth
living creature like *an eagle* in
flight" (Revelation 4.7). Another of John's

visions, this one of God's delivering power: "But the woman was given the two wings of the great *eagle* so that she might fly from the serpent into the wilderness" (Revelation 12.14).

Care to guess what the official emblem of the Roman army was? Yes, the golden eagle standard. Jesus was combining ideas here—where the dead are (animals or humans) birds of prey and scavenger birds gather. The scavenger birds, in this case, are the Roman soldiers, carrying before them the staffs topped with golden eagles. Josephus tells us that, just as Antiochus Epiphanes had, more than 200 years earlier, sacrificed a pig to Zeus on the altar of Jehovah, in A.D. 70 the Roman soldiers placed the eagle standard at the altar and made a sacrifice to the Emperor, hailing him as God Almighty.

Chapter Seven
The Stars Will Fall
From The Sky

The Bible has some weird things to say about the stars. Try this one on for size: "From heaven the stars fought, from their courses they fought against Sisera" (Judges 5.20). What exactly does that *mean*? Or how about this one: "[Where were you] when the morning stars sang together and all the sons of God shouted for joy?" (Job 38.7). What does *that one* mean? I'm seriously asking you these questions—when the Bible seems to personalize the stars, what in the world is it talking about?

The ancients (all of them), did, by the way, see the heavenly bodies as possessing heavenly souls. They connected the stars and planets with the angelic beings who served

God. Nowadays we understand cosmology in a much different framework than did *everyone* before the 1600s. C.S. Lewis has written a book (my favorite of all his writings) detailing the ancient and medieval understanding of the cosmos—*The Discarded Image*—and even as a modern man he was hesitant to give up the sheer beauty of the ancient view of the universe. If you have read Lewis' *The Voyage of the Dawn Treader*, you may remember the episode (in chapter 12) when Eustace encounters a living star/angel/heavenly-being:

> "In our world," said Eustace, "a star is a huge ball of flaming gas."

> "Even in your world, my son, that is not what a star is, but only what it is made of."

Signs In the Sky

The first mention of heavenly bodies in the Bible tells us that they are given as *signs*. "And God said, 'Let there be lights in the expanse of the heavens to separate the day from the night. And let them be for *signs* and for seasons, and for days and years, and let them be lights in the expanse of the heavens to give light upon the earth.' And it was so. And God made the two great lights—the greater light to rule the day and the lesser light to rule the night—and the stars" (Genesis 1.14-16).

Throughout the Old Testament, the Sun, Moon, and stars become symbols of people, tribes, and nations. One example is the bizarre dream that Joseph had: "Then he dreamed another dream and told it to his brothers and said, 'Behold, I have dreamed another dream. Behold, the sun, the moon, and eleven stars were bowing down to me.' But when he told it to his father and to his brothers, his father rebuked him and said to him, 'What is this dream that you have dreamed? Shall I and your mother and your brothers indeed come to bow ourselves to the ground before you?' And his brothers were jealous of him, but his father kept the saying in mind" (Genesis 37.9-11). Perhaps Joseph should have kept the dream to himself, because his sharing it sure stirred up trouble. Notice that his father *rebuked* him because he interpreted the dream as referring to *people*—specifically to him and his family.

The Old Testament prophets use images of cosmic chaos to describe the downfall of nations. In all the prophetic warnings, *the imagery of heavenly turmoil is never taken literally*! Some examples...

Isaiah prophesying against Babylon, which fell in 539 B.C.: "Behold, the day of the LORD comes, cruel, with wrath and fierce anger, to make the land a desolation and to destroy its sinners from it. For the stars of the heavens and their constellations will not give their light; the sun will be dark at its rising, and the moon will not shed its light" (Isaiah 13.9-10).

Amos, prophesying against Samaria, which fell in 722 B.C.: "'And on that day,' declares the Lord GOD, 'I will make the sun go down at noon and darken the earth in broad daylight. I will turn your feasts into mourning and all your songs into lamentation; I will bring sackcloth on every waist and baldness on every head; I will make it like the mourning for an only son and the end of it like a bitter day. Behold, the days are coming,' declares the Lord GOD, 'when I will send a famine on the land—not a famine of bread, nor a thirst for water, but of hearing the words of the LORD. They shall wander from sea to sea, and from north to east; they shall run to and fro, to seek the word of the LORD, but they shall not find it'" (Amos 8.9-12).

Ezekiel, prophesying against Egypt, which was besieged by Babylon for 40 years, from 571 to 531 B.C.: "When I blot you out, I will cover the heavens and make their stars dark; I will cover the sun with a cloud, and the moon shall not give its light. All the bright lights of heaven will I make dark over you, and put darkness on your land, declares the Lord GOD" (Ezekiel 32.7-9).

Joel's prophesy is fulfilled on the Day of Pentecost and quoted in full by Peter in his first sermon: "And it shall come to pass afterward, that I will pour out my Spirit on all flesh; your sons and your daughters shall prophesy, your old men shall dream dreams, and your young men shall see visions. Even on the male and female servants in those days I will pour out my Spirit. And I will show wonders in the heavens and on the earth, blood and fire and columns of smoke. The sun shall be turned to darkness, and the moon to blood, before the great and awesome day of the LORD comes. And it shall come to pass that everyone who calls on the name of the LORD shall be saved. For in Mount Zion and in Jerusalem there shall be those who escape, as the LORD has said, and among the survivors shall be those whom the LORD calls"(Joel 2.28-32).

When Peter quotes Joel as the text for his sermon on the Day of Pentecost, he says, "This is what was uttered through the prophet Joel" (Acts. 2.16). The King James Version is more emphatic: "*This* is *that* which was spoken by the prophet Joel." He then proceeds to quote, not just the text referencing the outpouring of the Spirit, but the *whole text*, including the lines about cosmic chaos. It was all fulfilled in the outpouring of the Holy Spirit, because *part* of what Pentecost was about was judgment on the house of Israel for rejecting the Messiah.

Paul confirms this in 1 Corinthians 14 (the chapter about speaking in tongues), when he quotes Isaiah 28 and shows that tongues are a sign of judgment against the unbelieving Jews: "In the Law it is written, 'By people of strange tongues and by the lips of foreigners will I speak to this people, and even then they will not listen to me, says the Lord.' Thus tongues are a sign not for believers but for unbelievers, while prophecy is a sign not for unbelievers but for believers" (1 Corinthians 14.21-22).

When the unbelieving people of Jerusalem heard the miracle of speaking in tongues on the Day of Pentecost, they mocked the disciples and accused them of being drunk, showing that "even then they will not listen to me." In their rejection of Jesus as Messiah and Lord they sealed their own fate. This was confirmed by their actions on the Day of Pentecost, and for them, the sun darkened and the moon turned to blood—the fate of the nation was set in concrete.

In Matthew 24, Jesus described the downfall of Israel like this:

"Immediately after the tribulation of those days the sun will be darkened, and the moon will not give its light, and the stars will fall from heaven, and the powers of the heavens will be shaken" (Matthew 24.29).

Jesus wasn't speaking literally, any more than Ezekiel or Joel or Amos was. In fact, he was lifting a phrase straight out of Isaiah 13, and by using the language of cosmic collapse he was poetically and prophetically saying that the powers of Israel—her Sun, Moon, and stars—her civil and spiritual government—were all headed for destruction.

By the way, we still use language like this in our poetry and music.

Billie Holiday, Stars Fell On Alabama: "We lived our little drama, we kissed in a field of white, and stars fell on Alabama tonight."

U2, The Fly: "It's no secret that the stars are falling from the sky, The universe exploded 'cause of one man's lie."

The Doors, Touch Me: "I'm gonna love you till the stars fall from the sky for you and I." (Bad grammar, I know, but you get the point).

The Sign of the Son of Man in Heaven

Jesus continues his warning by saying that the destruction of the Temple will be proof positive that he is Lord, and enthroned in heaven:

> "Then will appear in heaven the sign of the Son of Man, and then all the tribes of the earth will mourn..." (Matthew 24.30).

Sigh. The next few verses get tough. Translation is a tricky thing, even in the best of texts. Take a text that offers options, and it can get awkward. It is almost impossible to not include one's bias in the translation. Let me give you an example from this verse.

About half the translations (ESV, NIV, NASB, NKJV) say something like, "Then will appear in heaven [or in the sky] the sign of the Son of Man." Translating it this way, the thing that appears in heaven (or in the sky) is the sign, not the Son of Man.

The other half of the translations (KJV, ASV, RSV, D-R) say something like, "Then will appear the sign of the Son of Man in heaven." Translating it this way, a sign is given that the Son of Man is in heaven.

Either way of translating the text is correct. We have to choose. If the text means "the sign will appear in heaven," then we have to figure out what the sign is, and I'll leave that to you because I'm too busy reading it the other way. It makes more sense, to me, in this context, to translate it, "then there will appear a sign—a proof—a confirmation—that the Son of Man is in heaven."

Understood this way, the destruction of the Temple and the city of Jerusalem, and all the ensuing chaos not only in Israel but throughout the known Roman world, is evidence that Jesus is who he said he was, and that he has been exalted to the right hand of the Father and sits as Lord and King on the heavenly throne. The *sign* that the Son of Man is in heaven—and is who he claimed to be—is the very fulfillment of all the things he prophesied. He wasn't some crackpot when he laid claim to being Messiah, and this was confirmed by his words being fulfilled precisely when he said they would—in his own generation—with the downfall of Jerusalem.

One more translation difficulty. The verse continues, "and all the *tribes* of the earth will mourn." The NIV does a lousy job of translating here and says, "and all the *nations* of the earth will mourn." The word (*phule*) means tribes or clans, not nations, which has another word (*ethnos*). The difficulty, though, is with the word "earth." In Greek the word is *ge* (Get it? As in *ge*ology and *ge*ography?), and it means a multitude of things just like the English word earth does. When we say earth (or *ge*), do we mean the clump of dirt that we are holding in our hands, or the piece of ground that we are standing on, or the whole planet? Context is everything. Follow me carefully.

First, we're talking *tribes*, not *nations*. That's a no-brainer (*nations* is just a bad translation). Now, if you are from the United States and you say the word tribes in that context, you automatically think of Native

American Indians—Cherokee, Apache, Comanche, Navajo. But imagine for a minute that we are not talking about the context of North America, and are instead talking about the context of, oh, say, Israel! In that context, how shall we interpret *ge*? Shall we go for, "all the tribes of the whole world," or for, "all the tribes of *the land*"? The people of Israel—the twelve tribes—the sons and daughters of Abraham—are uniquely tied to "the land"—"the Promised Land." The word *ge* is, in fact, the word used in the New Testament for *The Land* that God promised: "and [God] said to [Abraham], 'Go out from your *land* and from your kindred and go into the *land* that I will show you'" (Acts 7.3).

Got it? Let's read it again: "And all the tribes of the Land will mourn." Of course they would mourn—their beloved Temple and City are no more. Whether these Jewish people were nearby—in the hillsides of Judea, or far off—in Spain or Britain or Rome—when news reached them of the destruction of the Temple, their hearts would be torn from their chests and they would rip their clothes in grief. This was unimaginable to them.

Coming On The Clouds Of Heaven

Verse 30 continues,

"and they will see the Son of Man coming on the clouds of heaven with power and great glory."

Jesus didn't just make up this line out of the clear blue. He is, again, quoting the Old Testament. And we can't understand it without looking at the Old Testament passage from which it was lifted. Of course, first century Jews who were deeply schooled in the prophets wouldn't have to study this out; it would instantly come to their understanding when they heard the phrase.

The first time the phrase is used is by prophet Daniel: "I saw in the night visions, and behold, *with the clouds of heaven there came one like a son of man,* and he came to the Ancient of Days and was presented before him. And to him was given dominion and glory and a kingdom, that all peoples, nations, and languages should serve him; his dominion is an everlasting dominion, which shall not pass away, and his kingdom one that shall not be destroyed" (Daniel 7.13-14).

Perhaps you have heard this text used for sermons about the Rapture, or the Second Coming. But look closely at the words. To *where* is the Son of Man coming? Orientation is everything! He is coming to "the Ancient of Days," that is, to God, the Father. This is not a picture of his coming *to earth*, it is a picture of his coming *to heaven*. Now, answer another question. When, in the whole of biblical history from Genesis to Revelation, does the Son of Man, surrounded with clouds, "come to the Father"? Obviously the answer is at the Ascension of Christ.

The Ascension is perhaps the most overlooked event in the life of Jesus. Too many people tend to see it simply as his, "exit, stage left"—as how he got out of the picture so the Holy Spirit could come on the Day of Pentecost. But the Ascension was the coronation day for King Jesus. He was led into the presence of the Father, and given dominion and glory and a kingdom. He was set upon the Throne of God as King of Kings and Lord of Lords. He formally began his rule, that "all peoples, nations and languages should serve him."

When Mark describes this event, he writes, "So then the Lord Jesus, after he had spoken to them, was taken up into heaven and sat down at the right hand of God" (Mark 16.19), and Luke tells us, "And when he had said these things, as they were looking on, he was lifted up, and a *cloud* took him out of their sight" (Acts 1.9).

The Ascension of Jesus (along with the Resurrection) was vindication of all that he said and did. The sign that the Son of Man was in heaven was the destruction of the Temple. In the destruction of the Old Covenant, they "saw" the reality of his enthronement. The one who was enthroned on the clouds at his Ascension, would, in that same generation, visit them with clouds of judgment.

Clouds of Judgment

Jesus was borrowing Daniel's language when he spoke of "the Son of Man coming on the clouds," but the other prophets were quick to use the language of clouds as language of judgment. Here are a few examples:

Psalm 104.1-3: "You are clothed with splendor and majesty, covering yourself with light as with a garment, stretching out the heavens like a tent. He lays the beams of his chambers on the waters; *he makes the clouds his chariot; he rides on the wings of the wind."*

Isaiah 19.1: "An oracle concerning Egypt. Behold, the LORD is *riding on a swift cloud* and comes to Egypt; and the idols of Egypt will tremble at his presence, and the heart of the Egyptians will melt within them."

Nahum 1.3: "The LORD is slow to anger and great in power, and the LORD will by no means clear the guilty. *His way is in whirlwind and storm, and the clouds are the dust of his feet."*

Jesus uses this same language in another passage in Matthew, which has given fits to interpreters trying to figure out who could possibly live from the time of Jesus until the Second Coming: "For the Son of Man is going to *come* with his angels in the glory of his Father, and then he will repay each person according to what he has done. Truly, I say to you, there are some standing here who will not taste death until they see *the Son of Man coming in his kingdom"* (Matthew 16.27-28). Again, when we read this as a description of the Ascension and subsequent fall of Jerusalem, it all makes sense.

Jesus says much the same thing when he stood before the high priest at his trial: "And the high priest stood up and said, 'Have you no answer to make? What is it that these men testify against you?' But Jesus remained silent. And the high priest said to him, 'I adjure you by the living God, tell us if you are the Christ, the Son of God.' Jesus said to him, 'You have said so. But I tell you, *from now on you will see the Son of Man seated at the right hand of Power* and *coming on the clouds of heaven*'" (Matthew 26.62-64). The high priest wasn't going to live to see the Second Coming. But he and his generation did see the Ascension, the outpouring of the Spirit on the Day of Pentecost, the explosion of the Gospel throughout the world, and the destruction of the Temple and Jerusalem.

He Will Send Out His Angels

This book is not my first eschatological rodeo. I have been studying and teaching on an eschatology of hope for over 25 years. I have taught retreats to congregations, I have led seminars, and—perhaps the most fun—I have sat one on one with pastors who, for some reason or another, wanted to discuss the subject with me. And it is at this point in the study that I hear something like, "OK...I'm not totally convinced of what you're saying, but it makes a lot of sense. But *don't tell me* you think this *next* verse was fulfilled in the first century!" I always take a deep breath, say, "Yep, I do," and jump into the next thing Jesus says. So, take a deep breath, hold on to your seat, and listen to the words of Jesus:

> *"And he will send out his angels with a loud trumpet call, and they will gather his elect from the four winds, from one end of heaven to the other" (Matthew 24.31).*

Once again, translation is an art, not a science. There are three important words in this verse: angels, trumpet-call, and gather. How we understand them completely determines how we understand what Jesus meant.

First, the word angels. The Greek word is *angelos*, and it means, simply, messenger. When we read it we automatically think it means something like "heavenly being," but it doesn't. Now, the heavenly beings *are* messengers of God, but they are not his only messengers. John the Baptist was a messenger of God. Jesus said of John the Baptist, "This is he of whom it is written, 'Behold, I send my *messenger* before your face, who will prepare your way before you'" (Matthew 11.10). Care to guess what the word translated messenger is? You got it—*angelos*! One more: "When the days drew near for him to be taken up, he set his face to go to Jerusalem. And he sent *messengers* ahead of him, who went and entered a village of the Samaritans, to make preparations for him" (Luke 9.51-52). Again, the word is the plural form of *angelos*.

The heavenly creatures are called cherubim and seraphim, thrones, powers, dominions and principalities—they are also called messengers, for they do God's bidding and speak for him. But God has other messengers as well. The Apostles and the 70 were the first messengers heralding the Gospel throughout Israel and throughout the world. Why, then, automatically read this verse as "He will send out his heavenly creatures..."? Why not read it, "He will send out his messengers"? This passage is a description of what Christ does with the early church. The last thing he says to them is, "Go into all the world"—he sent them out as messengers. In this verse he is describing what will happen—Jerusalem will fall, and with it the Old Covenant will end, but the messengers of God will go out into the whole world—"to the four winds, from one end of heaven to the other"—with the proclamation of the Gospel of King Jesus.

The second phrase—with a loud trumpet call—describes the action of the Apostles and the early evangelists. These men proclaimed a message that was *not* whispered in a corner. "What I tell you in the dark, say in the light, and what you hear whispered, proclaim on the housetops" (Matthew 10.27). Paul stood before Felix and said, "I am not out of my mind, most excellent Festus, but I am speaking true and rational words. For the king knows about these things, and to him I speak boldly. For I am persuaded that none of these things has escaped his notice, for this has not been done in a corner" (Acts 26.25-27). In Thessalonica, the pagans raged against the Christians, saying, "These men who have turned the world upside down have come here also" (Acts 17.6).

When God calls his own to himself, he does so with trumpets. "In that day from the river Euphrates to the Brook of Egypt the LORD will thresh out the grain, and you will be gleaned one by one, O people of Israel. And in that day a great trumpet will be blown, and those who were lost in the land of Assyria and those who were driven out to the land of Egypt will come and worship the LORD on the holy mountain at Jerusalem" (Isaiah 27.12-13). People in Assyria didn't literally hear a trumpet being sounded in Jerusalem.

But they were called out by God to gather to Zion and worship him.

We still use the imagery regarding an important announcement: "His speech was a clarion call for the nation." A clarion call is a direct public request for people to take action. The Gospel going forward is a clarion call for people to take action — to forsake their empty idols and false gods, and to follow the Lord of all — King Jesus.

And what will these messengers do, as they proclaim the Gospel as a clarion call? They will "gather his elect" from all over the world. This isn't a Rapture passage, about being caught away, it is an evangelism passage about harvesting souls and nations. The word gather is a combination of two Greek words, with both of which you will be familiar, because they have come over into our own language. The first is the prefix *epi* — we use it in epidural, epidermis, epicenter. It means "over." The second is *synagogue*, and it means, well, synagogue. It means "gathering." A Jewish synagogue is a gathering together of Jewish believers for worship. An English equivalent is "congregation."

This word, *episynagogue*, is used by Jesus when he weeps over the city of

Jerusalem and cries out, "O Jerusalem, Jerusalem, the city that kills the prophets and stones those who are sent to it! How often would I have *gathered* your children together as a hen *gathers* her brood under her wings, and you were not willing!" And then, apropos to our study, he finishes with this terrible line: "See, your house is left to you *desolate*" (Matthew 23.37).

Tellingly, the word is used again in the book of Hebrews: "And let us consider how to stir up one another to love and good works, not neglecting to *meet together*, as is the habit of some, but encouraging one another, and all the more as you see the Day drawing near" (Hebrews 10.24-25).

Now, let us revisit the verse in Matthew: Jerusalem is doomed to destruction, the stars are going to fall for the city, the Son of Man is going to come in judgment, because he is enthroned in the heavens as King and Lord, and he is also going to "send out his messengers with a loud trumpet call, and they will congregate—gather together— *episynagogue*—his elect all over the world."

Remember when we talked about the seed pod being destroyed, but first the seeds being dispersed? Before the Temple and the city could be judged, the Gospel had to go out —as a witness to the nations; the Apostles and early Christians had to go all over the world loudly proclaiming the Good News—and then the end would come.

This Generation

Just in case someone might hear him and think he was speaking of events a very long way off, Jesus finishes this section by saying,

> *"From the fig tree learn its lesson: as soon as its branch becomes tender and puts out its leaves, you know that summer is near. So also, when you see all these things, you know that he is near, at the very gates. Truly, I say to you, this generation will not pass away until all these things take place. Heaven and earth will pass away, but my words will not pass away" (Matthew 24.32-35).*

"*This generation* will not pass away until *all these things* have taken place." Which generation? *This* generation—the generation Jesus was speaking to. Not a generation 2000 years into the future (*a la* Hal Lindsay, Tim LaHaye, and company), but the people who were standing there listening to Jesus teach.

Everything Jesus described in this text about the Great Tribulation happened within 40 years of him speaking. Christians shouldn't be anticipating horrible days, growing wickedness, the rise of evil powers and an emergency rescue by a secret Rapture to get us out of here just in the nick of time. We should be looking for the accomplishment of the Great Commission, the triumph of the Church, and the Second Coming of Christ as a victory celebration.

Chapter Eight
As It Was
In The Days Of Noah

This is a book about the study of the end times, and so far we have spent seven chapters without talking about the end times! What we have addressed is hugely important —what is *not* the end-times but is mistakenly taken to be so by many. Everything we've studied so far in this book can be summed up in one sentence: "When Jesus described the 'Great Tribulation' in Matthew 24, he wasn't talking about something in *our* future, but something in *his hearers'* future, which occurred in three and a half years leading up to the destruction of Jerusalem in A.D. 70."

Now, we finally get to talk about *our* future—about what Jesus said regarding the Second Coming. But...

But...

I'm quoting Scripture here... "But..."

"But concerning that day and hour no one knows, not even the angels of heaven, nor the Son, but the Father only" (Matthew 24.36).

The Big But

I've spent a lot of ink explaining words in this book, but the smallest word of all needs the most explanation. If you don't want much detail, you can skip the next paragraph and just trust me when I say, it means a strong "but" which changes the subject of discussion. In other words, up until this verse, Jesus has been talking about what was going to happen less than a generation down the road. Now he *changes the subject* and talks about the Second Coming — *"But*, concerning *that* day and hour no one knows..."

The word translated "but" is the Greek word *de* (δέ for you Greek snobs, not to be confused with δή). It is a conjunction of antithesis, a marker of contrast. It serves to mark a transition to something new. It is universally used to denote opposition and distinction. It is a participle adversative. It opposes the thing previously mentioned and begins a new discussion. Oddly enough, it is sometimes translated "and," but there is always with it (even when it is "and") a degree of opposition and interruption. A.T. Robinson writes, concerning the use of this word in verse 36, "It is equally clear that in this verse Jesus has in mind the time of his second coming. He had plainly stated in verse 34 that those events (destruction of Jerusalem) would take place in that generation. He now as pointedly states that no one but the Father knows the day or the hour when these things (the second coming and the end of the world) will come to pass."[2]

With the opening word of verse 36, "but," Jesus shifts from talking about the destruction of Jerusalem to talking about the Second Coming. Notice the monumental difference in knowledge here. Regarding the soon-to-take-place events (everything he has described from verse 1 to 35) we have all kinds of data—goodness, we've spent six chapters looking at all the clues and warnings. But when it comes to the Second Coming, the radar goes blank. The sound waves go silent.

---

[2] Robertson, A. T., *Word Pictures in the New Testament* (Mt 24:36), Broadman Press, Nashville, 1932.

Nothing. "But concerning that day and hour no one knows, not even the angels of heaven, nor the Son, but the Father only." *No one knows* —this means every human being who ever lived, including the goofy radio and television preachers who prognosticate dates. *Not even the angels of heaven* —now we're not talking about human messengers, like we were a few verses back, but the *messengers of heaven.* The angels don't have a clue when Jesus is coming back. Ready for the bombshell? *Nor the Son!* Jesus, in his human limitations that he embraced in the Incarnation, was clueless about when he was returning. *Only the Father* knows, and he's not telling.

As It Was In The Days Of Noah

But there *is* something to know. Although Jesus doesn't know the *when* of his return, he does tell us the conditions of his return.

For as were the days of Noah, so will be the coming of the Son of Man. For as in those days before the flood they were eating and drinking, marrying and giving in marriage, until the day when Noah entered the ark..." (Matthew 24.37-38).

How was life in the days of Noah? In a word, normal. No Great Tribulation, no Antichrist, no plagues and earthquakes. No giant stinging scorpions. Life was normal. People were eating, they were drinking, they were marrying off their children. I have actually heard sermons where preachers said that the increase of people eating out in restaurants was a sign of the times! As if Jesus had said here, "Watch for this sign—there will be in *increase* of eating and drinking and marrying." The only thing we are promised an *increase* of is "his government and peace" (Isaiah 9.7). No, Jesus is here saying that, before his return, life will be going on as it always has gone on.

> *"...and they were unaware until the flood came and swept them all away, so will be the coming of the Son of Man. Then two men will be in the field; one will be taken and one left. Two women will be grinding at the mill; one will be taken and one left. Therefore, stay awake, for you do not know on what day your Lord is coming. But know this, that if the master of the house had known in what part of the night the thief was coming, he would have stayed awake and would not have let his house be broken into. Therefore you also must be ready, for the Son of Man is*

coming at an hour you do not expect" (Matthew 24.39-44).

These verses have provided more fodder for Rapture sermons than perhaps any text in the Bible. These verses are where the whole idea of "left behind" comes from! These verses are the go-to verses for folk who warn us to be sure we are Rapture-ready, because we certainly don't want to be left behind.

Well...I do. Yes, you read it right. I want to be left behind. Really. *Seriously.* I'm not being funny now, and there is no trick play on words. I hope to God I am left behind.

Look carefully at what theses verses are actually saying instead of what we have been told they are saying, and my guess is you will want to be left behind too. Follow the bouncing ball with these verses...

Bounce One: The times leading up to the Second Coming will be as it was in the days of Noah—life as normal.

Bounce Two: In the days of Noah, "they were unaware until the flood came and swept them all away." Question: *Who* was unaware? Was Noah aware that a flood was coming? Were his sons? His wife and daughters in law? Of course they were—they spent decades building a boat getting ready for the flood! So, when the text says *"they* were unaware," who is *they*? The wicked. If you are reading this in a room all by yourself, say it out loud—it will do you good—"the wicked." If you are in a room surrounded by other people you can say it out loud too, but you might get some strange looks. The wicked were unaware. *They* is speaking of *the wicked*.

The text tells us, "they were unaware until the flood came and swept them all away." *Who* was swept all away? Again, the right answer is, the wicked. So, re-read the verse fully understanding just who it is talking about: "[*The wicked*] were unaware until the flood came and swept [*the wicked*] all away."

Bounce Three (this is the *big* bounce): "so will be the coming of the Son of Man." The NIV translates this verse, "...and they knew nothing about what would happen until the flood came and *took them all away*. That is how it will be at the coming of the Son of Man." Look at the verse through new eyes and answer these questions: Who was taken away in the days of Noah? Who was left behind? "So will be the coming of the Son of Man."

"Then two men will be in the field; one will be taken and one left." Who gets taken? Who gets left? "As it was in the days of Noah, so shall it be at the coming of the Son of Man."

"Two women will be grinding at the mill; one will b taken and one left." Who gets taken? Who gets left? "As it was in the days of Noah, so shall it be at the coming of the Son of Man."

This is huge. This is a paradigm shift for people who were schooled to see this text as a Rapture reference. It isn't about being caught away at all, it's about been swept away in judgment. If you have, like me, read this verse as a Rapture verse for half your life, this re-seeing it takes some getting adjusted to. The brain is like a rubber band that tends to go back to its previous shape after being stretched. It takes a while. So, if you're learning about this interpretation for the first time, it's OK if your head spins for a while, and if you have to keep re-thinking it. But it really is as clear as clean glass when you look carefully at what the text is saying.

The principle this verse teaches is a principle about how God works, and so it is true whenever you apply it: *When God judges, he judges the wicked and the righteous are preserved and blessed*. Both at the end of history, and throughout history, when God judges, the wicked are "taken" in judgment, and the righteous are "left behind."

Reading It Like It's The First Time

Once a person sees what Matthew 24.39-41 is actually saying, and once that person understands the principle of judgment behind it, all kinds of Scripture suddenly start dovetailing and making sense like never before. Here are a few examples...

The Parable of the Wheat and Tare
Jesus told several parables, stories, to portray this principle of judgment, and to give a little insight into how judgment would work on the Last Day. The first is the Parable of the Wheat and Tare, or The Parable of the Weeds:

> *"He put another parable before them, saying, 'The kingdom of heaven may be compared to a man who sowed good seed in his field, but while his men were sleeping, his enemy came and sowed weeds among the wheat and went away. So when the plants came up and bore grain, then the weeds appeared also. And the servants of the master of the house came and said to him, 'Master, did you not sow good seed in your field?*

*How then does it have weeds?' He said to them, 'An enemy has done this.' So the servants said to him, 'Then do you want us to go and gather them?' But he said, 'No, lest in gathering the weeds you root up the wheat along with them. Let both grow together until the harvest, and at harvest time I will tell the reapers, **Gather the weeds first** and bind them in bundles to be burned, but gather the wheat into my barn'" (Matthew 13.24-30).*

Did you notice that, in the harvest described, the weeds are gathered *first*, then the wheat is harvested?

With most of his parables, Jesus leaves them unexplained. But he was gracious enough to expand on this one.

*"Then he left the crowds and went into the house. And his disciples came to him, saying, 'Explain to us the parable of the weeds of the field.' He answered, 'The one who sows the good seed is the Son of Man. The field is the world, and the good seed is the sons of the kingdom. The weeds are the sons of the evil one, and the enemy who sowed them is the devil. The harvest is the end of the age, and the reapers are angels. Just as the weeds are gathered and burned with fire, so will it be at the end of the age. The Son of Man will send his angels, and **they will***

*gather out of his kingdom all causes of sin and all law-breakers, and throw them into the fiery furnace. In that place there will be weeping and gnashing of teeth. **Then** the righteous will shine like the sun in the kingdom of their Father. He who has ears, let him hear"' (Matthew 13.36-43).*

When Christ comes again, it isn't to rescue the righteous and take them out, it is to bless and reward the righteous and take out the wicked (read that "take out" however you want to—I read it with a Don Corleone voice).

The Parable Of The Nets In the same chapter, Jesus tells a shorter story demonstrating the same principle.

*"Again, the kingdom of heaven is like a net that was thrown into the sea and gathered fish of every kind. When it was full, men drew it ashore and sat down and sorted the good into containers but threw away the bad. So it will be at the end of the age. The angels will come out and **separate the evil from the righteous** and throw them into the fiery furnace. In that place there will be weeping and gnashing of teeth" (Matthew 13.47-50).*

After the harvest, after the fishing trip, the wicked are taken away and the righteous are left.

Psalm 37 With this principle in mind, read Psalm 37 through new eyes.

¹ Fret not yourself because of evildoers; be not envious of wrongdoers!
*² For they will **soon fade** like the grass and wither like the green herb.*
³ Trust in the Lord, and do good; dwell in the land and befriend faithfulness.
⁴ Delight yourself in the Lord, and he will give you the desires of your heart.
⁵ Commit your way to the Lord; trust in him, and he will act.
⁶ He will bring forth your righteousness as the light, and your justice as the noonday.
⁷ Be still before the Lord and wait patiently for him; fret not yourself over the one who prospers in his way, over the man who carries out evil devices!
⁸ Refrain from anger, and forsake wrath! Fret not yourself; it tends only to evil.
*⁹ For **the evildoers shall be cut off**, but **those who wait for the Lord shall inherit the land**.*
*¹⁰ In just a little while, **the wicked will be no more**; though you look carefully at his place, he will not be there.*

11 But **the meek shall inherit the land** and delight themselves in abundant peace.

18 The Lord knows the days of the blameless, and their heritage will remain forever;
19 they are not put to shame in evil times; in the days of famine they have abundance.
20 But **the wicked will perish**; the enemies of the Lord are like the glory of the pastures; they vanish—like smoke they vanish away.

22 for **those blessed by the Lord shall inherit the land**, but **those cursed by him shall be cut off.**

28 For the Lord loves justice; he will not forsake his saints. They are preserved forever, but the children of the wicked shall be cut off.
29 **The righteous shall inherit the land** and dwell upon it forever.

34 Wait for the Lord and keep his way, and he will exalt you to inherit the land; you will look on **when the wicked are cut off.**
35 I have seen a wicked, ruthless man, spreading himself like a green laurel tree.
36 But he passed away, and behold, he was no more; though I sought him, he could not be found.
37 Mark the blameless and behold the upright, for there is a future for the man of peace.

³⁸ *But transgressors shall be altogether destroyed; the future of the wicked shall be cut off.*

Before coming to this understanding, the Beatitudes never made sense to me. What did Jesus mean, "Blessed are the meek, for they shall inherit the earth?" Of course, we Christians weren't going to inherit the earth. We were going to be taken *off* the earth, and the wicked would get it (remember the bumper sticker saying, "In Case of Rapture, You Can Have My Car"?). Oh, sure, we would come back after the Tribulation, at the Second Coming, and whip up on the wicked, and we would rule the earth for a thousand years, but that wasn't really inheriting it, because after the thousand years, it was all going to get blown to kingdom come. But now it all makes sense. The meek inherit the earth because the wicked are taken in judgment.

In A Little While

In Psalm 37.10, which we just read (you *did* read it, didn't you?), David sings, "In just a little while, the wicked will be no more." How long is a little while? God tells us, through Moses, when he gives Israel the Ten Commandments. "You shall not make for yourself a carved image, or any likeness of anything that is in heaven above, or that is in the earth beneath, or that is in the water under the earth. You shall not bow down to them or serve them, for I the Lord your God am a jealous God, *visiting the iniquity of the fathers on the children to the third and the fourth generation of those who hate me*, but showing steadfast love to thousands of those who love me and keep my commandments" (Exodus 20.4-6).

We will come back to Exodus in just a minute, but first let's take a short side trip to the book of Judges. Judges is a sad book. It tells about a series of leaders that God raised up to deliver his people every time they got themselves into a mess. Moses was dead. Joshua was dead. There "was no king in the land," and "every man did what was right in his own eyes." Consequently, the people of Israel fell into a vicious cycle that may sound familiar to you because you've seen it in your own life or in the life of others. First, they enjoyed a period of *silence*—they were serving God and things were peaceful. Then, they fell into *sin*, forgetting God and his ways. Because of this, God allowed some nasty neighbor to come in and oppress them and bring them under *servitude*. When they had had a stomach full of slavery or harassment, they cried out to God in *supplication*. In response, God would always raise up a judge, a *savior*, to deliver them. Then cycle would start all over again. The point to be made here is that when God's people (or any people) fall into wickedness, they cannot long endure.

Back to Exodus. Some people have misread this text and fretted that it taught the horrible doctrine that God would punish our children, grandchildren and great-grandchildren for our sins. Such a thing is contrary to the heart of God, who said, "Fathers shall not be put to death because of their children, nor shall children be put to death because of their fathers. Each one shall be put to death for his own sin" (Deuteronomy 24.16).

What the second commandment teaches is that God will put up with idolatry—with forsaking his ways—with evil, but he will put up with it for only so long, three or four generations at the most. If a nation or people or family walks in goodness, ethically, righteously, it will be blessed. But if it begins walking in treachery, evil, oppression, wickedness, it will be judged. The judgment may not happen today or tomorrow, but it will happen. As a rule, it will happen in three or four generations. Because of the consequences of its bad choices, the thing will crumble.

Judgment is worked in to the fabric of creation. How long is "a little while?" Three or four generations.

But—the same God who allows judgment to roll down on wickedness, promises that those who walk uprightly will enjoy his covenant blessings "for a thousand generations"—if you want to take that literally, for 40,000 years. But you know, it's not literal, it means for as long as the people walk in righteousness—forever, even.

The principle of judgment taught by Jesus in Matthew 24 (remember, that's what we were talking about way back at the beginning of the chapter—who gets taken and who gets left behind) and in the parables, the same principle which is born out throughout Scriptures including David and Moses, is this: God allows wickedness for a season, then he visits it and judges it and cuts it off,but the righteous flourish and endure. So it has been, so it is, and so it will be on the last day. Not a secret rescue operation from heaven, but the wicked being judged and the righteous inheriting the earth—the new earth, transformed at the return of Christ.

Left behind? My God, I hope so!

Chapter Nine
The Millennium...
Or Lack Thereof

Remember back in Chapter One, *The Battle Of The Views*, where we learned that all the eschatological views are labeled according to their view about the Millennium? Well, we've finally arrived at the subject itself. You may remember that there are three basic views: *Premillennial*, which teaches that Christ will return *before* the Millennium; *Postmillennial*, which teaches that Christ will return *after* the Millennium; and then the easy way out, *Amillennial*, which teaches that there *is no literal Millennium*, that the thousand years represents the time between Christ's First Coming and his Second Coming (the Church Age), and that Christ will return on the Last Day to set things right and make all things new. I say, if the easy way out is the right way out, take it every time.

Look! It's A Picture Book!

The book of Revelation (in which the Millennium passage is contained) is a book of pictures—symbols. Some people keep insisting that we interpret it literally: "If it says a thousand years it means a thousand years. Son, you can't be reading the Bible symbolically, that will get you into all kinds of trouble." But then, those same people go right ahead and read Revelation symbolically. For example, Revelation talks about a seven headed dragon rising up out of the sea (Chapter 13). *No one* takes that literally, not even the "literalists." "Oh, well that's a picture of a future world government composed of ten nations which were formally the Roman Empire—that's the revised Roman Empire which will be ruled by the Antichrist." My response is, "Man, can't you at least be consistent with the literalism you insist we all embrace? I think it's a real seven headed dragon coming up out of the sea—I think there's a movie about it co-starring King Kong." Then there's the "Whore of Babylon" in chapter 17. Some of the literalists tell us this is the Roman Catholic Church (*no, it isn't!*). I say, if we're going to insist on the 1000 years being literal, let's insist on the prostitute being literal too — so, there's this woman, dressed in red, who drinks a lot and rides on the back of a dragon. Cool.

You get my point, I hope. The book of Revelation is not a literal book, any more than the book of Psalms is literal when it talks about God having wings. The Bible is a collection of books (73 books and letters, written in two different languages, over a course of two thousand years, from three continents, by dozens of authors, under the inspiration and direction of the Holy Spirit), and each book has to be approached in terms of its own genre. There is story, poetry, prophecy, eye-witness history, personal correspondence, and more. We can't go insisting that everyone read everything in the Bible as if it were all the same genre.

The Number 1000

Given that the book of Revelation is unquestionably symbolic, how do we deal with this passage?

"Then I saw an angel coming down from heaven, holding in his hand the key to the bottomless pit and a great chain. And he seized

the dragon, that ancient serpent, who is the devil
and Satan, and bound him for a thousand
years, and threw him into the pit, and shut it
and sealed it over him, so that he might not
deceive the nations any longer, until the
thousand years were ended. After that he must
be released for a little while" (Revelation
20.1-3).

First, let's look at how the number 1000 is used in the rest of the Bible.

In Exodus, God tells us that he will judge wickedness soon, but show mercy for a long time: "for I the Lord your God am a jealous God, visiting the iniquity of the fathers on the children to the third and the fourth generation of those who hate me, but showing steadfast love to *thousands* of those who love me and keep my commandments" (Exodus 20.5-6). The ESV give us "thousands," other translations (NIV, GWT, GNT, NLT, NRSV, TNIV), give us "a thousand generations." The *New International Reader's Version* even says, *"But for a long time* to come I show love to all those who love me and keep my commandments."

Here's my question: we know that God visits iniquity in the third or fourth generation, but how long does he show mercy and lovingkindness to those who love him and keep his commandments? A thousand generations, the Bible tells us. Does this mean that the thousand and first generation comes along, and they too love God and keep his commandments, but they're just a little late to get in on the blessings? "Sorry," God says, "I really wish I could bless you too, but you just missed the deadline of my grace."

Of course not! "A thousand generations" in Exodus means, "*all* the generations"—every generation until the end of history. Just for fun, add this passage into the mix: "He remembers his covenant *forever*, the word that he commanded, for *a thousand generations*" (Psalm 105.8). Forever—for a thousand generations.

As a completely sarcastic side note, for those who *do* insist on the number 1000 being literal, a thousand generations is something like 40,000 years. God gave this promise 3000 years ago. Does that mean we have 37,000 years before everything wraps up? "No!" they respond, "In Exodus the number 1000...is...uh...symbolic." Check.

In Psalm 50.10 we read, "For every beast of the forest is mine, the cattle on *a thousand hills*." For three and a half years I pastored a wonderful congregation in St.

Croix County, Wisconsin. Most of the folk in the congregation were dairy farmers. Cows were everywhere. You'll never guess what St. Croix County called itself! "The County Of A Thousand Hills." So, is this Psalm saying that God owns all the cattle in St. Croix County? Just how many cattle does God own on how many hills? He owns *all* the cattle on *all* the hills in the world. Checkmate.

If we went on a camping trip and ended up in a swampy setting, we might pitch our tent, and then as the sun began to set, you might walk inside and say, "Man, there are *a million* mosquitos out there!" But you didn't really count them, and you don't really know how many mosquitos are out there. What you meant is, "Goodness, there are a *bunch* of mosquitos out there...I think every mosquito in the world is right outside the tent door!" A Jew, in the first century, would have walked into the tent and exclaimed, "Oy vey! There are *a thousand* mosquitos out there."

When the book of Revelation says that Satan is bound for a thousand years, it simply means "a bunch of years"—it means "all the years."

And so you might respond, "Don't tell me you think Satan is bound *now*!" Yes, that's exactly what I'm about to tell you.

The Binding of Satan

The book of Revelation tells us that Satan will be bound—specifically, he will be bound, "that he might not deceive the nations any longer"—for a thousand years; for all the years. But John, in his Revelation, is not the first to use this kind of language. Jesus used it before him. "And the scribes who came down from Jerusalem were saying, 'He is possessed by Beelzebul,' and 'by the prince of demons he casts out the demons.' And he called them to him and said to them in parables, 'How can Satan cast out Satan? If a kingdom is divided against itself, that kingdom cannot stand. And if a house is divided against itself, that house will not be able to stand. And if Satan has risen up against himself and is divided, he cannot stand, but is coming to an end. But no one can enter a strong man's house and plunder his goods, unless he first *binds the strong man*. Then indeed he may plunder his house'" (Mark 3.22-27).

The point Jesus was making was this— by setting free a demon-possessed man, he was plundering the very house of Satan. But how can a strong man's house be plundered unless the strong man is first tied up—*bound*? In the very acts of his many exorcisms, Jesus was proving that he had authority over Satan, that he had tied him up, and was setting his captives free. The Matthew parallel reads, "But if it is by the Spirit of God that I cast out demons, then *the kingdom of God has come upon you*" (Matthew 12.28; cf. Luke 20.17-20). Put the two versions together: *the binding of Satan is the coming of the Kingdom of God.*

In the Gospel of Luke we read a story about the 70 disciples coming back rejoicing that the demons submit to them in Jesus' name. Jesus responded, "*I saw Satan fall* like lightning from heaven. Behold, I have given you authority to tread on serpents and scorpions, and over all the power of the enemy, and nothing shall hurt you" (Luke 10.18-19). In the next chapter, Jesus tells his disciples, "When a strong man, fully armed, guards his own palace, his goods are safe; but when one stronger than he attacks him and *overcomes* him, he takes away his armor in which he trusted and divides his spoil" (Luke 11.21-22).

In the Gospels, Jesus was on a mission to bind, bring down, overcome, plunder, and destroy Satan and his power. Speaking of his imminent death on the cross, Jesus said, *"Now is the judgment of this world; now will the ruler of this world be cast out.* And I, when I am lifted up from the earth, will draw all people to myself (John 12.31-21).

Eight chapters before John speaks of the binding of Satan, he has a vision which describes the thing in different imagery:

> *"And a great sign appeared in heaven: a woman clothed with the sun, with the moon under her feet, and on her head a crown of twelve stars. She was pregnant and was crying out in birth pains and the agony of giving birth. And another sign appeared in heaven: behold, a great red dragon, with seven heads and ten horns, and on his heads seven diadems. His tail swept down a third of the stars of heaven and cast them to the earth. And the dragon stood before the woman who was about to give birth, so that when she bore her child he might devour it. She gave birth to a male child, one who is to rule all the nations with a rod of iron, but her child was caught up to God and to his throne, and the woman fled into the wilderness, where she has a place prepared by God, in which she is to be nourished for 1,260 days."*

"Now war arose in heaven, Michael and his angels fighting against the dragon. And the dragon and his angels fought back, but he was defeated, and there was no longer any place for them in heaven. **And the great dragon was thrown down,** *that ancient serpent, who is called the devil and Satan, the deceiver of the whole world*—**he was thrown down** *to the earth, and his angels were thrown down with him. And I heard a loud voice in heaven, saying, "Now the salvation and the power and the kingdom of our God and the authority of his Christ have come, for* **the accuser of our brothers has been thrown down,** *who accuses them day and night before our God. And they have conquered him by the blood of the Lamb and by the word of their testimony, for they loved not their lives even unto death. Therefore, rejoice, O heavens and you who dwell in them! But woe to you, O earth and sea, for the devil has come down to you in great wrath, because he knows that his time is short" (Revelation 12.1-12).*

What a dramatic portrayal of the Virgin Mary giving birth to the Son of God, his Ascension into heaven, and as a result, a throwing down of Satan! Satan has lost his power to accuse us (because of the sacrifice of Christ on the cross for our sins). He has lost his power to rule us (because of the descent of

Christ into hell, where he wrested from Satan the keys to death, hell and the grave; and because of his glorious Resurrection and Ascension). He still tries to do his dirty work in the earthly region, but "he knows that his time is short"—he knows his opportunity for working evil is limited. And it keeps getting shorter and more limited as the militant Church of Jesus Christ moves forward in victory.

It All Started In Genesis

There is a little four-fold pattern of approaching the events in the Bible which is very helpful in understanding the workings of God. The pattern, briefly, is this:

•**Promised:** God prophetically promises to do something.

•**Provided:** God does what he promised, in a definitive way.

•**Progressive:** God continues to unfold what he has begun.

•**Perfected:** In the end, the deed is done in fullness, to completion.

The promised things usually have their beginning in Genesis, and most of the imagery in the Bible can be traced back to that book. Revelation talks about the dragon, "that old serpent", but the imagery of Satan as the serpent goes all the way back to Genesis 3.

Let's look at the binding, conquering, crushing, and plundering of Satan through the lens of this fourfold pattern.

Promised: In Genesis 3.15 God promises the serpent, in the hearing of the newly fallen Eve, that she will have a son who will set things right: "I will put enmity between you and the woman, and between your offspring and her offspring; he shall bruise your head, and you shall bruise his heel." This passage is called the *Protoevangelion* —the "first Good News." But the good news carries with it some pain. This Son of Eve will crush the head of the serpent, but his heel will get bruised in the process.

Provided: The definitive fulfillment of this promise happened at the cross. Jesus' "heel" was bruised—but it was "a mere flesh wound," and in that selfsame moment, his heel came down hard on the head of the serpent and crushed it: "And you, who were dead in your trespasses and the uncircumcision of your flesh, God made alive together with him, having forgiven us all our trespasses, by canceling the record of debt that stood against us with its legal demands. This he set aside, nailing it to the cross. *He disarmed the rulers and authorities and put them to open shame, by triumphing over them in him"* (Colossians 2.13-15).

Progressive: What occurred definitively in the death and resurrection of Jesus continues to unfold in the life of the Church. Satan was bound in the ministry of Christ. He is bound all the more as the Church accomplishes her mission of making disciples of the nations. He was crushed under the foot of Jesus, but, "The God of peace will soon *crush Satan* under *your* feet" (Romans 16.20).

Perfected: On the Last Day, when Christ returns to his victorious Church, Satan and all his powers, and everything which opposes God, will be finally and fully defeated: *"Then comes the end,* when he delivers the kingdom to God the Father after *destroying every rule and every authority and power.* For he must reign until he has put *all his enemies under his feet.* The last enemy to be destroyed is death" (1 Corinthians 15.24-26).

One of the problems with the Premillennial view is that it tends to subjugate the promised victories and blessings of the Church into some time-after-time distant future. But the promises of God are for *this* time and *this* place. He has called us, in the here and now, to walk in victory, or, to borrow the language from Revelation 20.4, to come to life and reign with Christ for a thousand years.

Chapter Ten
The First Resurrection

Premillennialists have really cool charts —full color and filled with dragons and stinging scorpions (think John Hagee on the tube, or if you're old enough and lived in the South, John Hall traveling the country with his massive painting; and if you've never read Clarence Larkin's *Dispensational Truth*, you owe it to yourself right now to put this book down, Google it, and look at the amazing graphics created nearly 100 years ago. Literally.). Of course the charts are incredibly complicated, but this just serves to show that us regular folk can't quite grasp the depth of understanding held by the teachers.

One of the things all the charts have is a timeline of *two* resurrections. The first resurrection happens at the Rapture, right before the seven year Great Tribulation. Then there's the thousand year space of the Millennium, and then there's the second resurrection, when everybody who didn't make it in the Rapture rises from the dead for Judgment Day.

These charts come from an interesting reading of Revelation 20:

"They came to life and reigned with Christ for a thousand years. The rest of the dead did not come to life until the thousand years were ended. This is the first resurrection. Blessed and holy is the one who shares in the first resurrection! Over such the second death has no power, but they will be priests of God and of Christ, and they will reign with him for a thousand years" (Revelation 20.4b-6).

Amillennialists, on the other hand, have boring charts. Ours just show one arrow up. At THE Resurrection, on the Last Day.

The Two Resurrections

Literalists insist that there are two physical resurrections. The first resurrection is of the believers who rise at the Rapture. The second resurrection is at the end of history.

But, wait a minute. Doesn't the Bible have a lot to say about *spiritual* resurrection? What if the first resurrection is our spiritual resurrection—being born again—and the second resurrection is our physical resurrection on the Last Day?

When Paul describes what happened to us when we were born again into the Kingdom of God, he says, "And you were *dead* in the trespasses and sins in which you once walked...But God, being rich in mercy, because of the great love with which he loved us, even when we were *dead* in our trespasses, *made us alive* together with Christ—by grace you have been saved -and raised us up with him and seated us with him in the heavenly places in Christ Jesus" (Ephesians 2.1-6).

We were dead. Now we're alive. What do you *call* that? You call it a resurrection.

In the Gospel of John, Jesus uses the same language. Pay careful attention to what he says: "Truly, truly, I say to you, whoever hears my word and believes him who sent me has eternal life. He does not come into judgment, but *has passed from death to life.* Truly, truly, I say to you, an hour is coming, and *is now here*, when the *dead* will hear the voice of the Son of God, and those who hear will *live*" (John 5.24-25).

Jesus tells us that the one who believes on him *has* (past tense—has already) passed from death to life. This is not a description of the future; Jesus says the time *is now here* when *dead* people will hear his voice and *live*.

What do you call a dead person passing from death to eternal life? You call it a resurrection.

The first resurrection is spiritual rebirth in Jesus Christ. That is when we come to life —to real life. That is when we begin reigning with Christ. That is what John is describing in Revelation 20: "They came to life and reigned with Christ for a thousand years." When we are born again we come to life, and Paul tells us we are "seated with him in heavenly places in Christ Jesus" (Ephesians 2.6). We are seated with Christ—enthroned. We reign with him in the here and now. In the thousand years.

John writes, "blessed and holy is the one who shares in the first resurrection! Over such the second death has no power." Blessed indeed! The first death is physical, and we all die. The second death is spiritual (eternal condemnation), and it has no power over those who are in Christ. Instead, the Revelation tells us, we are *"priests* of God and of Christ" and we will *"reign* with him for a thousand years." Priests who reign — a royal priesthood. In the here and now. Peter wrote, "But you *are* a chosen race, a *royal priesthood*, a holy nation, a people for his own possession, that you may proclaim the excellencies of him who called you out of darkness into his marvelous light" (1 Peter 2.9).

If the first resurrection was a spiritual one, which we have already experienced, and are consequently priests of God who rule and reign with Christ, then the second resurrection is a physical one which happens *on the Last Day.*

Back to what Jesus was saying in John 5. We've already looked at verse 24-25, but read it again so you'll get the flow of the next thing Jesus says: "Truly, truly, I say to you, whoever hears my word and believes him who sent me *has* eternal life. He does not come into judgment, but *has passed from death to life.* Truly, truly, I say to you, an hour is coming, and *is now here*, when the *dead* will hear the voice of the Son of God, and those who hear will *live*." Being born again. Spiritual resurrection. The first resurrection.

Now, verse 28-29: "Do not marvel at this, for an hour *is coming* when *all who are in the tombs* will hear his voice and come out, those who have done good to the resurrection of life, and those who have done evil to the resurrection of judgment." Physical resurrection. Judgment Day. The second resurrection.

The Bible teaches *a single physical resurrection of everybody*—the just and the unjust —in one fell swoop. Some inherit eternal life, some don't. But it all happens at the same time.

The prophet Daniel wrote, "And many of those who sleep in the dust of the earth shall awake, some to everlasting life, and some to shame and everlasting contempt" (Daniel 12.2).

When Lazarus died, his sister Martha approached Jesus and said, "'Lord, if you had been here, my brother would not have died. But even now I know that whatever you ask from God, God will give you.' Jesus said to her, 'Your brother will rise again.' Martha said to him, 'I know that he will rise again in *the resurrection on the last day*'" (John 11.21-24).

Jesus could have taken this as a grand opportunity to correct Martha's erroneous view of the end times. "Oh, Martha — Lazarus loved me. He won't rise in the resurrection on the last day, no, honey, he'll rise in the Rapture, a thousand and seven years before the last day!" But of course, Martha wasn't wrong (and at the death of a loved one is a bad time to discuss theological fine points anyway). She understood exactly what Daniel and everyone else understood: there is a general resurrection of everyone — the righteous and the unrighteous — on the Last Day. But Jesus did go ahead and bring up the whole idea of *spiritual* resurrection: "I am the resurrection and the life. Whoever believes in me, though he die, yet shall he live, and everyone who lives and believes in me shall never die. Do you believe this?" (John 11.25-26).

Paul falls right in line with Daniel, Martha and Jesus: "So is it with the resurrection of the dead. What is sown is perishable; what is raised is imperishable" (1 Corinthians 15.42). Did you notice? *The* resurrection of the dead. Singular. One resurrection. On the Last Day. In the book of Acts, when Paul stood trial before Felix, he said, "But this I confess to you, that according to the Way, which they call a sect, I worship

171

the God of our fathers, believing everything laid down by the Law and written in the Prophets, having a hope in God, which these men themselves accept, that there will be a resurrection of both the just and the unjust" (Acts 24.14-15). *A* (singular) resurrection of *both* the just and the unjust.

The first resurrection is spiritual, being born from above into the Kingdom of God. The second resurrection is physical, and happens to all of us on the Last Day, when Christ returns.

The chart just got a lot simpler to draw.

Chapter Eleven
A Word About Revelation

In the last chapter we looked at
Revelation 20, and since so many people think
the book of Revelation is about eschatology, I
suppose it would be a good thing to give the
whole book a chapter.

Let me begin by saying what you are
probably expecting me to say anyway. The
book of Revelation is not about eschatology.
Not any more than the books of 1 Corinthians
or 1 Thessalonians or Matthew or Acts. It has
some eschatology in it, but it isn't *about*
eschatology. It's about covenant.

Let me also get this out of the way:
most of this chapter is going to be plagiarized.
I'm taking the bulk of it from a book on the
Ten Commandments written by a witty,

handsome, thoughtful author. You can read more about the subject in that book.[3]

The Power of Story

Before we talk about the Book of Revelation, let's talk for a minute about movies and good stories. I'm going to share with you two quick ones.

The first is set in a dusty Old West town somewhere out in the rough mountains of Texas. The small village is beset by a tough gang of outlaws who have taken control of the place. The people of the town are having their lives ruined by the bad guys. The gang rides into town, causing havoc, shooting up the place, leaving dead bodies in the street, disrupting the peaceful life of the good citizens. Unexpectedly, a hero appears, but he doesn't look like a hero. He has weaknesses, is kind hearted, and seems puny. But he shows bravery and takes on the bad guys. At first it looks like he's going to lose, but the tables turn and he cleans up the town and restores peace. Of course, the prettiest maiden in the village falls in love with him and they get married and

[3] Kenneth N. Myers, *How Christians Behave*, Denison, TX, Mayeux Press, 2010.

have children and live together happily ever after.

The next story is set in some far-flung galaxy in an imaginary science fiction time of "a long, long time ago." The planet of peace-loving people find themselves taken over by an evil intergalactic force which disrupts their lives and runs roughshod over them. Unexpectedly, an unlikely young hero with a lightsaber and a fast spaceship shows up. At first everyone agrees he is a nobody — a nothing — but then they see he is really the champion. He fights against the evil empire, almost loses his life, but in the end destroys their gigantic starship and liberates the people. And there is a love story here, too.

Did you notice the similarities? The only basic difference is between six-shooters and laser swords, fast horses and flying machines. The fact that the stories are basically the same is not an accident. It is called a *meta-story* — the same basic tale, told in a different setting. Most good stories share a kind of common DNA.

Speaking of DNA, did you know that the code for your entire bodily make-up is contained in every single cell of your body? I am no expert on DNA, but here is what I know: the basic data of your body is contained, like a little computer program, in every fiber of your being. Scientists can take a cell from anywhere in your body and find all the information they need about who you are: your skin color, your hair and eye color, your basic propensity for diseases and weaknesses, your family relations, and everything else about you.

The DNA Of The Bible

Just like the good stories having a *meta-story*, and just like your body having DNA in every cell, the Bible has a kind of DNA that is woven throughout the whole thing. Once you see it, you see it everywhere. It is called the *covenant model*,[4] and whereas your body's DNA has a long and complicated string to it, the Bible's DNA has only five points. I am convinced that if you were to make an effort to memorize the five points of covenant, you would suddenly find yourself making a lot more sense of the Bible, from Genesis all the way through to Revelation.

---

[4] What follows may be found in detail in Ray Sutton's *That You May Prosper*, Dominion Press, Fort Worth, TX, 1987. I count this as one of the five books that have changed my life, and I highly recommend it to you.

To set the stage for the five points of covenant, let me share one more story. A great and powerful king of a world empire—let's say the king of ancient Babylon, or Persia, or Rome—arrives to rescue a small nation from the hand of some evil despot. After freeing the people from the oppressor, he offers to make covenant with them. It doesn't matter where you turn in ancient literature, the covenant model was always the same. First, the king establishes that he is the one in charge (there is no bargaining here; it is a take it or leave it deal). Second, he names and puts in place the leadership which will represent him. Third, he lays out clearly and in writing what is expected of the people. Fourth, he details what will happen if the people keep their end of the deal, and what will happen if they don't. Fifth and finally, the king makes it clear how the covenant continues into the future—how new generations reaffirm the covenant, how new leadership is installed. Simple enough? OK, now let's dig in.

Transcendence

The first point of covenant is called *transcendence*. In this section of the covenant, the king firmly establishes that he is the one in charge. He is transcendent—above and beyond—the situation. In a very real sense, he isn't a player in the game, he is over and above the game. He determines the rules. The question asked in this first point is, "Who makes the rules?" And the answer is, "The king makes the rules. The transcendent one calls the shots."

Hierarchy

The second point of covenant is called *hierarchy*. The great king has no intention of hanging around in the smaller country for the rest of his life. He is going back to his palace, hanging gardens, and servants. But, he is going to leave someone there to officially represent him—someone to speak on his behalf. It may be his son, the prince, or it may be an appointed governor, but whoever it is, this person (or these persons) carries the very authority of the king with them. They can't make the rules (only the king can do that), but they can see to it that the king's rules are followed. The question asked in this second point of covenant is, "Who enforces the rules?" And the answer is, "The king's appointed hierarchy enforces the rules set by the king."

Ethics

The third point of covenant is called *ethics*. In this section of the written, signed, and sealed covenant, the king clearly states what is expected of the people in order for them to keep this covenantal arrangement with the king. This is the section where all the rules are clearly spelled out. These rules are not subject to debate, nor are they arrived at by some kind of democratic process or some bargaining deal-making. The king simply says, "I am the one in charge, and if you are going to walk in covenant with me, here is what you have to do." The question asked in this third point of covenant is, "What are the rules?" And the answer is, "The rules are whatever the king says they are."

Sanctions

The fourth point of covenant is called *sanctions*. In the covenant document, all the consequences of keeping the rules or breaking the rules are spelled out clearly. There can be no real covenant without consequences. The biblical language of sanctions is "blessings and curses." The blessings and the curses come, not arbitrarily, but as the consequences of the people honoring the covenant made. If the people keep the covenant, "all these blessings" come upon them. If they break the covenant, "all these curses" come upon them. The question asked in this fourth point of covenant is, "What are the consequences of keeping or breaking the rules?" And the answer is, "The consequences of keeping the covenant are these blessings, and the consequences of breaking the covenant are these curses."

Continuity

The fifth point of covenant is called *continuity*. The final thing all these ancient covenants establish is how the covenant continues into the future. Sooner or later the king is going to die, so when his son, the prince, becomes the king, how is the covenant renewed? Or, when the children of the original covenant people grow up, how do they renew the covenant with the king? This is also called the *succession clause*. The question asked in this fifth point of covenant is, "How does this covenant continue into the future?" And the answer is, "This covenant continues by future generations renewing and keeping the covenant."

Covenant in the Bible

I wish I could take time here to write an entire detailed book on how the Bible is full of this covenant model. But then, that would be a completely different book from this one, and it has already been written anyway, by a far better writer—Bishop Ray Sutton's *That You May Prosper.* So, for the moment, let me show you just a few places where this covenant model comes into play in the Bible.

- It is found in the original mandate given by God to Adam (Genesis 1 & 2).

- It is found as the structure of the Pentateuch, the first five books of the Bible.

- It is, particularly, the structure of the book of Deuteronomy.

- It is the basic model for most, if not all, the books of the prophets, who were themselves covenant representatives reminding Israel that God had established covenant with them and they were breaking it.

- It is the structure of the Gospel of Matthew.

181

• It is the structure of the book of Romans.

These are only a handful of the places you will find this model in the pages of the Holy Scriptures, but the *last* place you will find it in the Bible is in the book of Revelation.

Covenant And The Book Of Revelation

The book of Revelation is clearly a covenant document. It is not a book of *revelations* (plural), but a book of *"The revelation* of Jesus Christ, which God gave him to show to his servants the things that must soon take place" (Revelation 1.1). This book has been, especially in our own time, a much misunderstood prophecy, with modern day hucksters trying to interpret it with the Bible in one hand and a newspaper in the other. People have tried to read into it whatever current situation they found themselves in, missing entirely the point made in the first verse—it was given to show what "must soon take place." Soon, in a first-century context, not a twenty-first-century one.

Here is a very brief outline of the book of Revelation:

Transcendence (Chapter 1): In which John has a vision of the transcendent Lord, the "alpha and omega," the "beginning and the end." John sees Jesus as the King of kings who establishes the new *covenant* (and hence a new five points of covenant).

Hierarchy (Chapters 2 and 3): in which letters are written to the *angels*—the *messengers* (Greek: *angelos*)—the bishops—of the emerging new covenant people. In particular, Jesus is speaking to the bishops under the Apostle John's care in Asia Minor.

Ethics (Chapters 4 and 5): in which we see the throne room scene in heaven, where the Lamb of God opens the seven-sealed scroll (a seven-sealed scroll was a covenant document—a will—sealed by seven witnesses). Here is declared the new ethic for the Church. I would also point out that in this scene the Lamb alone is worthy to open this New Covenant and establish it with his people, and what follows is worship and praise around the throne of God with consequent results in the earth below.

Sanctions (chapters 6 through 19): in which we find the negative consequences of breaking the covenant poured out upon unfaithful Israel. The bulk of the book is a detailing of these curses, which mimic the curses poured out upon Egypt in the book of Exodus—now being poured out upon a singularly called out nation; a bride, who became a whore (the "whore of Babylon," I would suggest, is Israel, riding on the back of the beast of Rome); a covenant people who chose to reject the Messiah and instead join league with Caesar—the "Beast" who was soon turn and devour her, destroying all that was sacred—the Temple and the City.

Continuity (Chapters 20 through 22): in which a new covenant people emerge from the downfall of ancient Judaism—the "bride of Christ," the "heavenly Jerusalem," the Church of Jesus (cf. Hebrews 12.22-24).

The book of Revelation is not, primarily, about our future. It is about the future of the generation that saw Jesus in the flesh. It was written to encourage the struggling, newly emerging Church to endure to the end and to have hope that victory was theirs. While there is application for our lives and our future (just as with any other book of the Bible), it was written to show "what must soon take place." This book is not a crystal ball through which we gaze in search of nuclear holocausts and an emerging evil world leader.

It is a covenant document, spelling out the *demise of the Old Covenant* — "In speaking of a new covenant, he makes the first one obsolete. And what is becoming obsolete and growing old is ready to vanish away" (Hebrews 8.13) —and the establishing of the New Covenant made with us by our Lord Jesus Christ.

Chapter Twelve
What Are We Waiting For?

This is the last chapter in a book about eschatology—the study of last things—and other than a few pages about the resurrection, we still haven't *really* studied any last things. What we have done in the bulk of our time together is take a whole lot of things that others have put in the caboose—in the last car of the train—and brought them up toward the engine where they belong. The Great Tribulation doesn't belong at the end of the Gospel story, it belongs at the beginning. The Antichrists (plural) don't belong at the end either—in the "last hour" of the Old Covenant John wrote, "many antichrists have come" (1 John 2.18). The Millennium doesn't belong at the end of the story, either. It belongs, depending on how you want to look at it, either nowhere or everywhere in the New Covenant era (literally it doesn't fit anywhere, figuratively it fits everywhere).

So, what *does* happen in the future? I thought you'd never ask.

The Future Of The World

To say it briefly, the Bible teaches that the world will turn to Christ—isn't that why he came, to give his life for the *life of the world*? The Great Commission will be accomplished —I still don't understand how people can be OK with the idea that Christ would give his Church a mandate, give them the power to accomplish the mandate, and then then make eschatological promises that the Church will fail miserably at its calling. The expectations of the prophets from long ago will be fulfilled —what Isaiah and Daniel and Ezekiel and others saw was not a picture of some history after history, but the unfolding of God's plan in real world history.

Here, then, are some Scripture promises about our future, which we should work for and expect to see before the end (some, if not most, of these have been relegated to a future millennium by popular end-times teachers):

- Psalm 86.9: *"All the nations* you have made shall *come and worship* before you, O Lord, and shall glorify your name."

- Psalm 2.7-8: "I will tell of the decree: The Lord said to me, 'You are my Son; today I have begotten you. Ask of me, and *I will make the nations* your heritage, and *the ends of the earth* your possession.'"

- Daniel 2.34-35, 44 (Daniel describes and interprets a dream King Nebuchadnezzar dreamed): "As you looked, a stone was cut out by no human hand, and it struck the image on its feet of iron and clay, and broke them in pieces. [35] Then the iron, the clay, the bronze, the silver, and the gold, all together were broken in pieces, and became like the chaff of the summer threshing floors; and the wind carried them away, so that not a trace of them could be found. But *the stone* that struck the image *became a great mountain and filled the whole earth*...And in the days of those kings the *God of heaven will set up a kingdom that shall never be destroyed*, nor shall the kingdom be left to another people. It shall break in pieces all these kingdoms and bring them to an end, and *it shall stand forever.*"

- Isaiah 9.6-7: "For to us a child is born, to us a son is given; and *the government shall be upon his shoulder*, and his name shall be called Wonderful Counselor, Mighty God, Everlasting Father, Prince of Peace. Of the *increase of his government and of peace there will be no end*, on the throne of David and over his kingdom, to establish it and to uphold it with justice and with righteousness from this time forth and forevermore. The zeal of the Lord of hosts will do this."

- Isaiah 11.9: "They shall not hurt or destroy in all my holy mountain; for *the earth shall be full of the knowledge of the Lord as the waters cover the sea.*"

- Malachi 1.11: "'*For from the rising of the sun to its setting my name will be great among the nations*, and in *every place* incense will be offered to my name, and a pure offering. For *my name will be great among the nations*,' says the Lord of hosts."

As the nations turn to Christ, the blessings of peace and prosperity and longevity — the blessings of walking in covenant with God — will be poured out. The prophets use beautiful poetic language, like "the wolf shall lie down with the lamb," to describe a future of peace and blessings *for the whole world*, as it follows after Christ.

- Isaiah 2.4: "He shall judge between the nations, and shall decide disputes for many peoples; and they shall beat their swords into plowshares, and their spears into pruning hooks; *nation shall not lift up sword against nation*, neither shall they learn war anymore."

- Isaiah 65.19-25: "'I will rejoice in Jerusalem and be glad in my people; no more shall be heard in it the sound of weeping and the cry of distress. No more shall there be in it an infant who lives but a few days, or an old man who does not fill out his days, *for the young man shall die a hundred years old, and the sinner a hundred years old shall be accursed*. They shall build houses and inhabit them; they shall plant vineyards and eat their fruit. They shall not build and another inhabit; they shall not plant and another eat; for like the days of a tree shall the days of my people be, and my chosen shall long enjoy the work of their hands. They shall not labor in vain or bear children for calamity, for they shall be the offspring of the blessed of the Lord, and their descendants with them. Before they call I will answer; while they are yet speaking I will hear. The *wolf and the lamb shall graze together*; the *lion shall eat straw like the ox*, and *dust shall be the serpent's food*. They shall not hurt or destroy in all my holy mountain,' says the Lord."

• Revelation 15.4: "Who will not fear, O Lord, and glorify your name? For you alone are holy. *All nations will come and worship you*, for your righteous acts have been revealed."

The future of the world is not dystopian, one huge bad landscape of evil. It will become, under the blessings of God, a place of goodness, bounty and peace. This is not to say that all evil will cease or all sin will be banished — remember the four-step process in Chapter 9: Promised, Provided, Progressive, Perfected. The world will not become perfect until the New Creation, but its *orientation* is in that direction.

192

The Future Of The Church

How can such a future world possibly come to be? Only as it turns to God and follows his ways. But how can the world turn to God and follow his ways without the Church proclaiming his ways to every tribe, tongue, and nation? And how can the Church accomplish this amazing feat of the Spirit's power unless the Church itself matures, grows in love, and becomes one? What does the Bible say about the future of the Church?

The Church will become one, fulfilling Jesus' prayer in John 17: "I do not ask for these only, but also for those who will believe in me through their word, *that they may all be one*, just as you, Father, are in me, and I in you, that they also may be in us, so that the world may believe that you have sent me. The glory that you have given me I have given to them, that they may be one even as we are one, I in them and you in me, that they may become perfectly one, *so that the world may know* that you sent me and loved them even as you loved me" (John 17.20-23). Jesus asked his Father for this. Will the Father refuse his request? In fact, wasn't this the Father's idea to begin with? He said to the Son, "Ask of me, and *I will make the nations* your heritage, and *the ends*

of the earth your possession" (Psalm 2.8).
Didn't God the Father *send* the Son for the
world's sake? "For God so loved *the world*, that
he gave his only Son, that whoever believes in
him should not perish but have eternal life.
For God did not send his Son into the world
to condemn the world, but *in order that the world
might be saved through him*" (John 3.16-17).

The Church will become united in faith,
fulfilling the very reason that God gave us
spiritual leadership: "And he gave the apostles,
the prophets, the evangelists, the shepherds
and teachers, to equip the saints for the work
of ministry, for building up the body of Christ,
until we all attain to the unity of the faith and of
the knowledge of the Son of God, to mature
manhood, to the measure of the stature of the
fullness of Christ" (Ephesians 4.11-13). Notice
the "until" in this text? Paul has the full
expectation that the Bride of Christ will
become united and mature.

The Church will become mature and
pure, a Bride appropriate for her Bridegroom:
"Husbands, love your wives, as Christ loved
the church and gave himself up for her, that he
might sanctify her, having cleansed her by the
washing of water with the word, *so that he
might present the church to himself in splendor*,
without spot or wrinkle or any such thing, that

she might be holy and without blemish" (Ephesians 5.25-27).

In a word, the Church will become everything God has called her to become, and will accomplish everything God had directed her to accomplish. For people involved in the world of the Church today, this seems far-fetched. We can only dream of it! But dream we must, and work toward, and never give up. It is the will of God, and it is the destiny of the Church.

The Future of Israel

Dispensationalists make the nation of Israel into God's timepiece. Their teaching goes like this: Israel was restored as a nation in 1948, and that started the countdown clock ticking. Within a generation of 1948 (hey—we're there, already!), the Rapture will happen. Now—get this: *after* the Church is taken off the planet a revival breaks out Israel begins to Christ, and 144,000 Jews follow Jesus and proclaim his Lordship. But the Antichrist will break his covenant with them, wreak havoc on them, and put them to the sword. At the end of the Great Tribulation, when Jesus returns, they will finally believe in their Messiah, and those who didn't get wiped out in the Tribulation will get to live during the Millennium. In short, the Dispensationalist future for Israel is not a rosy one.

Here is a more hopeful view: Israel, in the context of our time and history, will come to Christ and enjoy all the benefits of walking in covenant with him. In Peter's second sermon (his first was on the Day of Pentecost), speaking to the people of Israel, he said, "And now, brothers, I know that you acted in ignorance, as did also your rulers. But what God foretold by the mouth of all the prophets, that his Christ would suffer, he thus fulfilled. Repent therefore, and turn back, that your sins may be blotted out, that times of refreshing may come from the presence of the Lord, and that he may send the Christ appointed for you, Jesus, whom heaven must receive until the time for restoring all the things about which God spoke by the mouth of his holy prophets long ago" (Acts 3.17-21).

Notice the fourfold process of Israel returning to Christ:

1. **Repent:** "Repent therefore, and turn back..." Israel turns to Christ as a result of the Gospel being proclaimed.

2. **Refreshing:** "...that times of refreshing may come from the presence of the Lord..." Because Israel turns to Christ, she enjoys the refreshing presence of the Lord, the covenant blessings that are hers in Abraham.

3. **Return:** "...that he may send the Christ appointed for you, Jesus, whom the heavens must receive until the time..." The conversion of the nations, and the conversion of Israel usher in the return of Christ. Until then, "the heavens must receive [retain]" him.

4. **Restoration:** "...until the time for restoring all the things about which God spoke by the mouth of his holy prophets long ago." All the promises of God spoken over Israel come to fruition in the New Creation. Paul wrote about that restoration in Romans: "For I consider that the sufferings of this present time are not worth comparing with the glory that is to be revealed to us. For the creation waits with eager longing for the revealing of the sons of God. For the creation was subjected to futility, not willingly, but because of him who subjected it, in hope that the creation itself will be set free from its bondage to corruption and obtain the freedom of the glory of the

children of God. For we know that the whole creation has been groaning together in the pains of childbirth until now. And not only the creation, but we ourselves, who have the firstfruits of the Spirit, groan inwardly as we wait eagerly for adoption as sons, the redemption of our bodies. For in this hope we were saved" (Romans 8.18-24). Creation itself is standing on tiptoe anticipating the resurrection of believers, because in that day, creation too will be made new. All things will be restored.

God hasn't forgotten about his chosen people Israel. He has a New Covenant plan for her. That plan is not lived out separately from the Church (as the Dispensationalists would have us believe—Israel turning to God *after* the Church disappears), but with and as part of the Church. In Romans 11, Paul, who loves Israel so much he says he wishes he himself could go to hell on her behalf, describes God's plan for her with another fourfold pattern (Let the reader understand— this is *really good stuff*! So wade through it carefully and pay close attention):

1. **Israel is not rejected:** "I ask, then, has God rejected his people? By no means! For I myself am an Israelite, a descendant of

Abraham, a member of the tribe of Benjamin. God has not rejected his people whom he foreknew" (Romans 11.1-2). God hasn't forgotten about Israel.

2. **A remnant of Israel follows Christ** in Paul's day: "So too at the present time there is a remnant, chosen by grace. But if it is by grace, it is no longer on the basis of works; otherwise grace would no longer be grace" (vv. 5,6). The Apostles were Jews. The first multitudes to follow Jesus were Jews. The 120 in the Upper Room on the Day of Pentecost were Jews. 3000 Jews came to Christ that very day. Throughout history many Jews have continued to welcome Christ as their Messiah and are reconciled to him, not by works, but by grace.

3. **All Israel will be saved:** "So I ask, did they stumble in order that they might fall? By no means! Rather through their trespass salvation has come to the Gentiles, so as to make Israel jealous. Now if their trespass means riches for the world, and if their failure means riches for the Gentiles, how much more will their full inclusion mean" (vv. 11-12). Paul tells us (in v. 26), "in this way all Israel will be saved." Through seeing the blessings of God poured

out on the Church, and receiving the Gospel of grace, the whole nation will turn again to Christ. All Israel will be saved, just like all Mexico will be saved and all America will be saved and all Saudi Arabia will be saved! Now, here's the stunning part. Paul says their stumbling meant "riches for the world" and their failure meant "riches for the Gentiles." What riches, you ask? The riches of the Gospel; the riches of reconciliation with God; the riches of being grafted in to Abraham and made the people of God; the riches of salvation. But—the restoration of Israel to God will bring about "much more" riches. What could possibly be richer than being given the Gospel, reconciliation with God, and the gift of salvation? Only. One. Thing...

4. **Resurrection:** "For if their rejection means the reconciliation of the world, what will their acceptance mean but *life from the dead*?" (v. 15).

How is *that* for a timepiece? The nations come to Christ, Israel comes to Christ, Christ comes to Israel and all nations!

The Second Coming

The last thing in history as we know it is the return of Christ. We just saw where Peter preached in Act 3, that Jesus "must remain in heaven until the time comes for God to restore all things..." This verse alone squashes the Rapture/Tribulation/2nd Coming/Literal Millennium idea. He must remain in heaven until the restoration of all things. The last thing on the timeline is the return of Christ.

Paul lays out the scenario clearly: "But in fact Christ has been raised from the dead, the firstfruits of those who have fallen asleep. For as by a man came death, by a man has come also the resurrection of the dead. For as in Adam all die, so also in Christ shall all be made alive. But each in his own order: Christ the firstfruits, then at his coming those who belong to Christ. Then comes the end, when he delivers the kingdom to God the Father after destroying every rule and every authority and power. For he must reign until he has put all his enemies under his feet. The last enemy to be destroyed is death. For 'God has put all things in subjection under his feet.' But when it says, 'all things are put in subjection,' it is plain that he is excepted who put all things in subjection under him. When all things are subjected to him, then the Son himself will also be subjected to him who put all things in subjection under him, that God may be all in all" (1 Corinthians 15.20-28).

A Meeting In The Air

OK, OK, already! Some of you have been sitting on pins and needles wanting to ask, "But what about 1 Thessalonians and our being 'caught up to meet the Lord in the air?'" Here's your answer. It will happen. At the Second Coming and not a second before.

But what is immensely important is the *reason* for the catching up — the meeting is the big deal, and not the transportation for getting to the meeting. If we think the catching up is to whisk us away, we completely miss the point. The catching up is to get us to the meeting.

The word translated "meet" is *apantesis*, and it has a very special meaning. It is used on three occasions in the Bible. The first is in the story Jesus told about the Ten Virgins, when the bridegroom is headed in to town and the cry goes out, "Here is the bridegroom! Come out to *meet* him" (Matthew 25.6). Don't think

for a moment that they were going out to meet
the bridegroom in order to go away with him.

The second place the word is used is
when Paul, in chains, along with Luke and
some others arrive in Rome. The Christians
there hear Paul and his company are arriving
and, "came as far as the Forum of Appius and
Three Taverns to *meet* us" (Acts. 28.15). Don't
think for a minute that these Roman
Christians were going out of the city to meet
Paul and go away with him.

The final place the word is used is the
passage we're looking at in 1 Thessalonians—
the one everybody has wanted to talk about
since about halfway through this book: "But
we do not want you to be uninformed,
brothers, about those who are asleep, that you
may not grieve as others do who have no hope.
For since we believe that Jesus died and rose
again, even so, through Jesus, God will bring
with him those who have fallen asleep. For
this we declare to you by a word from the
Lord, that we who are alive, who are left until
the coming of the Lord, will not precede those
who have fallen asleep. For the Lord himself
will descend from heaven with a cry of
command, with the voice of an archangel, and
with the sound of the trumpet of God. And the
dead in Christ will rise first. Then we who are

alive, who are left, will be caught up together with them in the clouds to *meet* the Lord in the air, and so we will always be with the Lord" (1 Thessalonians 4.13-17). Don't think for a minute that we're going out to meet the Lord so we can go away with him.

The word "meet" (*apantesis*) is a special word which means to go out to welcome an incoming dignitary. The virgins go out to welcome the bridegroom to the festivities. The Roman Christians go out welcome Paul to their city. All of us Christians (living and dead) on the Last Day, go out to welcome King Jesus home. And in that moment, heaven and earth will be made one. And the New Creation will have been completed. "And so we will always be with the Lord," Paul writes.

The New Creation

We have already seen Peter proclaiming "the restoration of all things" in Acts 3. John describes it as a new creation in Revelation:

> *"Then I saw a new heaven and a new earth, for the first heaven and the first earth had passed away, and the sea was no more. And I saw the*

holy city, new Jerusalem, coming down out of heaven from God, prepared as a bride adorned for her husband. And I heard a loud voice from the throne saying, 'Behold, the dwelling place of God is with man. He will dwell with them, and they will be his people, and God himself will be with them as their God. He will wipe away every tear from their eyes, and death shall be no more, neither shall there be mourning, nor crying, nor pain anymore, for the former things have passed away'" (Revelation 21.1-4).

When the end—the real end—comes, it is a new beginning. It isn't this whole creation scrapped and thrown away—"blown to kingdom come"—and brand spanking new creation replacing it. It is this creation made new! This is why Paul tells us in Romans that "the creation waits with eager longing for the revealing of the sons of God...in hope that the *creation itself will be set free* from its bondage to corruption and obtain the freedom of the glory of the children of God" (Romans 8.19-21).

This isn't the first time in the Bible we've seen talk of a new creation. The new creation was **promised** all throughout the Old Testament. It was **provided** in the Resurrection of Jesus (he is the "firstfruit" of this new creation). It **progresses** throughout history in the life of the Church—"Therefore, if anyone is in Christ, he is a new creation. The old has passed away; behold, the new has come" (1 Thessalonians 5.17); "For neither circumcision counts for anything, nor uncircumcision, but a new creation" (Galatians 6.15). And it will be **perfected**, brought to completion, when Christ returns.

This world made new. This world, joined to heaven, and our eternal home. I'll probably be down in the Yucatan. You should come visit sometime.

Recommended Reading

If the book in your hands has whetted your appetite for further study, I recommend these:

Chilton, David; *The Days of Vengeance: An Exposition of the Book of Revelation*; Fort Worth; Dominion Press; republished 2006. An amazing verse by verse commentary on the Book of Revelation; but a warning: some of the footnotes and appendices were written by someone other than the author, and are often mean-spirited.

Gentry, Kenneth L; *Before Jerusalem Fell: Dating the Book of Revelation*; 1998 (republished 2010); Victorious Hope Publishing. A convincing argument for the early date of the Book of Revelation.

Riddlebarger, Kim; *A Case for Amillenialism*; Grand Rapids; Baker Book House, 2003. A very good introduction and overview of the Amillennial position.

Wright, N.T., *Surprised By Hope*; San Francisco, HarperOne, 2008. A stunning and biblical look at the future and heaven.

About the Author

Kenneth Myers was born in 1959 in Denison, Texas. The son of a pastor/missionary, he married Shirley McSorley in 1977. They have three children and two grandchildren. He is an Anglican bishop and pastors Christ Church Cathedral in Sherman, Texas.

www.kennethmyers.net

Made in the USA
Columbia, SC
08 July 2017